THE MESSAGES

Scribed by

Barbara Lynn Veltri

Veltri, Barbara Lynn

The Messages

ISBN 978-0-9704020-1-1 (paperback)

1. Jeshua Teachings 2. Scribed words of Jesus

Photo credits:

Front Cover © Barbara Lynn Veltri

Back Cover © Barbara Lynn Veltri

Printed in The United States of America

In loving memory of Anthony Martin Ellis

a brilliant, kind, compassionate friend whose

magnificent smile, and Spirit-directed

purpose touched everyone he encountered.

Table of Contents

"Before I formed you in the womb, I knew you and approved of you as My chosen instrument."

- Jeremiah 1:5

"For I will not even presume to speak of anything except what Christ has done through me as an instrument in His hands."

- Romans 15:18

"The Lord said to him 'Go, for he is a chosen instrument of mine to carry my name before the Gentiles and kings and the children of Israel."

- Acts 9:15

"I am as necessary to God, as He is to me, for I am the channel to bring his plan to pass."

Florence Scovel Shinn - *Your Word is Your Wand*

INTRODUCTION

Dear One,

Greetings. It is I, Jeshua, and I am with you as you scribe my messages.

Do you not think it is possible that I come through you? Believe this to be so. The Messages apply to all and will awaken, uplift, comfort, and extend peace to hearts and souls.

The world, as you know it, is responding to changes in consciousness.

This Spirit consciousness is opening pathways for light and love to flow from beings of light to hearts and souls on your planet. Today I ask you to believe that The Renaissance of Souls is upon your Earth's plane and consider the reasons why I ask you to communicate my messages.

In *A Course in Miracles*, I spoke of matters to offer mind correction and forgiveness. At this time, messages you scribe offer a new series of thoughts and lessons that are less verbose, meant for human beings to read, reflect, listen to, and offer heart, mind, and soul healing.

It is time to clarify terms and meanings that, for too long, have seemed to serve a purpose other than God's. If one moves to greater clarity of mind by listening to and learning from universal truths presented here, all benefit. As one's inner demeanor changes, joy is spread outward to all one encounters.

Therefore, I request your attention to my messages and ask that you scribe when you sense my interaction with you. This work is important to all who share in The Oneness of The Father.

Breathe deeply, feel your soul connect with mine, and go in peace and love today. This Introduction and purpose statement concludes today's dictation.

J

MEDITATION

Quiet the mind.

Calm the racing heart.

Cease movement.

Close the eyes, Be silent.

Breathe easy.

Be still, Rest.

Listen, Hear the wind.

See the mountains.

Sense the touch of God's angels.

They surround your soul being.

Detach, Exhale.

At this moment, nothingness transcends being.

All that is - is.

And you, as a soul Being, are one with your Creator.

You are returned to your natural set-point, that is peace, calm, and Spirit-filled.

Amen.

J

1. PEACE WITHIN

Dear One,

My peace is with your peace today and all days. I speak today on peace.

Peace is a given. It is your natural state of SOUL SELF. Self-realization and self-discovery are merely a return to your peaceful self within, that never changes, is forever constant, and is present for all time.

Your peace is the calm within, your centering anchor, your True North. The peace within is the respite from perpetual endeavors and busyness that moves one away from centering.

I recognized the importance of centering Self and gave thanks to Source from whom my peace was rooted, as is yours. I didn't feel or recognize any of the emotional barriers to peace that your world seems to project as reality. I didn't feel pressure or guilt or a sense that I needed to do anything. I abided within the present moment, and always knew that Truth was and is True, and all else was an attempt to move my mind from the peace of God.

Being centered in God means to be centered in peace.

Peace is always your state of perfect self, your connection to The Divine. Peace is present, within, always, and it is your connection to me.

Peace doesn't need to be given - it is. Recognize this gift.

When you come from a peaceful centering, you are balanced, rooted in now, and less prone to emotional tilts and upheavals.

'You need do nothing' means that the peace within is always a part of you, and seeking for it is unnecessary. Be still, quiet the mind, and work to remove the self-imposed barriers that defend against finding peace where it is... within.

J

2. TRUST

Dear One,

Today, I wish to share a message on Trust, which is the unwavering belief in the Divine God, Father, Higher Power, Universal Mind, and Oneness. This is a simple truth. Trust, Faith, and Belief are absolutes. Always and eternal.

The trust of my fellow disciples vacillated, as ego used any opportunity to enter the mind, causing upset, doubt, worry, or thoughts of worst-case (on Earth's plane) scenario thinking.

At times, your trust teeters, like a child's way, seeking comfort for physical needs to be met or seeking evidence of answered prayer in the form of tangible results. But you do not know what anything is for, nor the lessons that each situation offers to your soul's growth.

In your world, we witness those who attempt to negotiate with God. Picking and choosing when and how to trust or sacrificing for an outcome.

Prayers seem ritualized and formatted by those who believe themselves to be "unworthy sinners" or supplicants in need.

Speak with gratitude, affirm your authentic connection to God who knows all - including your mind and heart.

In all things, know that you are a child of The Divine.

Stay centered in Spirit. Ask with absolute trust, and you shall receive.

Spirit knows your heart, mind, and soul, as do all the heavenly beings around you and your angel guides.

Guidance comes when your soul's light energy flows and is not blocked by worldly concerns.

In my time, sickness, heartache, famine, war, destruction, and low-level emotions of envy, pride, lust, gluttony, and fear reigned among those who espoused to be followers of The Law.

But the law was stretched to fit man's desires of the body and ego mind. For me, and my brethren, ordained with the Holy Spirit's light and love, after my Ascension:

Trust transfigured fear, faith transformed doubt, peace transcended worry, and joy filled formerly anxious hearts.

You are in a body to do good in your capacity to do so, as I have stated previously.

You are not on Earth's plane for eternity. Each human form will pass from this world when your soul enters the kingdom of heaven.

The worldly way of trusting is not The Father's way.

Trust unwaveringly. "Be still and know that I am God."

J

3. COLLECTIVE EGO

Dear One,

Collective ego is not of God. The collective ego influences your thought system from the day you are born. You are asked to choose between two primary beliefs, love, or fear, in every encounter with self and others.

Collective ego mind releases waves of fear-based thinking that paralyzes beings on Earth's plane.

Collective ego envelops many millions of minds across all nations. Collective ego influences minds that succumb to flawed belief systems.

Collective ego manipulates emotions, resulting in actions that are hurtful, demoralizing, and destructive.

Collective ego's manufactured ideas circulate across airwaves, media, gadgets, and voices that perpetuate deeper divides, greater instability, thoughts of intense fear, and confusion.

God's Direction is consistent, offers clarity to illuminate the path of the light worker, and supports acts of love and compassion.

Direction from Source penetrates the collective ego when you seek guidance. I sought refuge from the world in prayerful solitude.

So, I ask you, what if all that you hold onto in your world were taken away?

What would that mean?

Neither the wealthy nor powerful will remain in form forever. No one escapes their body's decay on Earth's plane.

There is no everlasting-body.

Perhaps it is worthwhile to reconsider the attachment to concerns that distract one from their true work in nature.

The true nature of the Universe is to be personally peaceful.

The peace of God within is The Father's gift to all sons and daughters.

Peace is the heart's desire of every being, regardless of their position or location across earth environs.

Choose a silent space, separated from collective ego beliefs. There, the peace of God will be with you.

There, you will discern the work that is yours to do.

You cannot take on the perceived challenges of others and maintain your personal peace.

Even enlightened beings detach from the world to regain their connection to the Spirit.

Through prayer, my mind was connected to the Source.

This is yours to do today and all days.

J

4. BALANCE

Dear One,

What do you do as your life's work? How do you reconcile your 'personal' agreement to enter form when Spirit brought your "self" to life, with the demands of the Earth world? How can you be of greatest service to others?

There is significance in each soul's recapturing their purpose, living a life they were destined to live, while manifesting compassion to every being across the Earth's plane.

Your perception of the world, community, family, and strangers you interact with, extends energies. Each form either extends fear, doubt, mistrust, love, kindness, or calm.

Take a break and close your eyes. Breathe and release three times. Be still.

Feel into the peaceful state where your soul connects to the Force of the One who created you.

Feel the comfort in the release of all that is not joy, peace, love, calm, or contentment.

There are instances in every minute and every place on Earth's plane where like-minded, light-filled souls Do Good in their capacity to do so.

Know that Divine Love heals, casts out fear, worry, judgment, and guilt. Know that Divine Love nulls comparison.

Know that The One Mind loved you before you assumed form.

This is constant, changeless, and unalterable.

The balance of energy on Earth begins and ends with you.

J

5. CALM (IN THE FACE OF CRISIS)

Dear One,

How can I reassure you that I am with you? In the most trying times, call out to Me. I am, as always, with you.

The human condition is not without pain, sorrow, and more. It is a time when calls are made to God- "God help me, God help us."

At times of heightened anxiety and calamity, in the absence of calm, I am with you and all.

The words that I share with you today focus on what is necessary to heal the planet and restore the human mind to alignment with the mind of God.

The individual who longs for comfort seeks more material goods and pleasures. The temporary thrill of a physical possession erodes with time and with a change in health and financial condition.

It appears that more people on the planet are impacted by natural disasters, economic instabilities, loss of loved ones, war, and images that undermine the true purpose of love, unconditional care, and devotion to others.

How did things get this way, you may ask?

Humanity moves in tides and cycles across the time continuum. The ages of early civilization strove to survive, and conquests determined the survival of some and the annihilation of others.

Shifts in Earth's physical form moved humankind to distant lands. Caught in the fray of worldly peril, innocent souls crossed together en masse, to the next plane. Not all souls who transition from Earth to the beyond, find peace in a harmonious garden of light.

They do find love, because at the deepest level, each soul returns to The Love that created them, from which they are.

The void felt within beings on Earth at this time and during others in human evolution, is one of concern, as ego mind messages permeate, polarize, and disempower the collective "mind."

Can you respond with greater care and empathy?

Can you model calm in the face of crisis?

Can you admit an error when you have wronged another and apologize?

Can you speak and act with grace to elevate the vibration in your everyday interaction with others?

Fear, angst, worry, and depression are examples of low-level consciousness. Messaging and perceptions from world-based thinking fester in undisciplined minds and manifest energies.

When this occurs, emotions trigger a roller coaster sensation: up one minute, down the next, over reactions, gossip, angst, and/or explosive arguments tend to surface, leading to fear-based action.

This is not the way of the soul.

This is not the way of love.

This is not the path to communion of spirit-filled consciousness. But there is a choice.

Changing the vibration of the planet begins with you. Go now as a renewed being of calm in the outer world. That is all.

J

6. RESPONSE and REPOSE

Dear One,

Today, I come to you to speak about Response. To respond requires the mind's considering a thought, perception, idea, person, or situation that connects to life on Earth. Response is a reactive state. It catapults a being into action. At times, the action that occurs as a holy instant supports a brother or sister.

But response can be impulsive, or a pre-meditated, planned action instigated by an emotional directive. Response often triggers the fight or flight mechanism in the human mind, that accompanies a "rush" of energy.

Response can result in mis-action or intervention that affects the doer and other recipients of the doing, in ways that result in angst, alarm, agitation, anxiety, and alienation – as one is disconnected from what is truly Real.

The ego mind is in a constant state of responding - to crises, companions, colleagues, curiosities, criticism, and campaigns. The response mechanism that does not emanate from love, is misguided, and initiated by one whose heart is blocked by a focused attention on fear-based thoughts and messaging that is not from God.

God's response is always Constant. God's response is always Loving.

The world's ego response is erratic and jarring. It can grow a seed into a weed that strangles the blossom of pure light and love energy. The world's ego response seeks to divide, disengage, destroy, and deny Truth.

The time it takes to respond, without considering what God's Truth is, can do harm to a person, community, country, and reputation.

The ego response will not bring peace or internal contentment. The ego response can, within a short Earth moment, trigger emotions of fear, anxiety, lack, consternation, and regret that results in accusations or decisions that are not grounded in truth or as Truth. Response requires constant motion, doing, or action.

Consider your own life and frame of mind when you are unbalanced. Stimuli can incite agitation, and agitation seeks a reaction.

The reaction, like a hill you climb in your mind, moves you to respond not from your right mind, but from a false self. It's not a pleasant hike, but a stressful exertion, cascading your being into a spiral that triggers response, after response, after response. These actions never end in peace until you pause and quiet your mind.

The pause is your real self, connecting with Source, the All-Knowing Light that silences the responses of the world. Pause realigns your being and resets your mind-meter to react with balanced responses to ego and worldly messaging.

Seek not to respond in haste, but seek first to listen, show compassion, and understand. When you ask The Father, "What will you have me do?"

You will be directed, and His response is for the good of all. You will feel peace.

You will feel love.

You will feel Repose.

Repose is the absence of Response.

Repose is God's reconnecting time with your mind. Be content to simply relax into the state of Repose that releases all emotions.

Does your heart still beat without your response?

Do your eyes still blink without your manipulation?

Consider the peace within that renews the soul that guides your right action as you live within a body in this lifetime.

J

7. IMPATIENCE

Dear One.

I come to speak to you about an emotion that is pervasive in your world. It contributes to much angst, body ailments, and un-wellness.

Impatience is the mind's way of wanting to control an outcome, speed up the process, or enable a worldly goal or action. This is an emotional push to make things happen and disrupts a natural flow.

The cycles of the moon, seasons, blossoms, ripening fruits on the vine, and patterns of geese flying overhead in formation in the sky, are always in perfect time.

It is man who feels compelled to play God by rushing a process, altering a form, and attempting to control time by rushing things along at a quickened pace.

The heavenly bodies in the sky and the kingdoms of creation on land and sea do not respond to attempts to control outcomes or natural flow.

Impatience is not a virtue.

Rather, it is a form of mind that insists on control. Immediacy is preferred over waiting for events, healing, or processes to unfold.

Impatience is a relative of anxiety, stress, and aggression. It creates disharmony and is the opposite of being fully present in the moment.

Desiring something now, often supposes that a human mind knows what's best, and one sets out to fulfill their wants immediately.

The antidote for impatience is stillness. Harmonize your being with the peaceful rhythm of your soul.

Rest in God. Pause, breathe, detach.

J

8. SELF IMPOSED BLOCKS TO LOVE

Dear One,

Your heart's desires can come to you if you are direct and honest with yourself. What do you really want? State and ask with clarity.

Why do you really want this? How can you achieve this outcome? If you examine these questions, the only roadblock is your own mind.

You create obstacles to change and self-transformation. You list issues (don't have time, too old, too young, too poor, too weak).

You create obstacles of space and location (can't go there, wouldn't know anyone, hard to pack up, don't want to leave family, job, friends).

You create limitations (the don't haves: money, good health, transportation, place to go, abilities, friends, youth, or age), and then there are what the mind views as IMAGE BLOCKERS (Not good enough, not attractive, not talented, not feeling my best, not smart).

And before you know it, the mind has closed the heart's capacity to accept self-love. How can one attract the Beloved, if you focus on the faults you perceive about yourself?

Exude happiness that radiates out to others.

Be the one that attracts like a captivating magnet. If you are critical of potential partners, there is something to examine about self-criticism.

All work on manifesting begins with the love of self. It is tough work because one does not want to examine the self that plays victim, martyr, saboteur, or judge.

One sees self as fine/OK on the surface, but when alone, the "self-talk" of mind, personality, and ego, destroys who you are - a child of God perfectly aligned to Spirit's love.

For today, *apologize to yourself for setting up blocks to your good.*

Call in guidance and truly make a promise to accept what comes to you without judgment.

Create time to communicate with your own Higher Guidance, to tap into a consistent flow, as you let go of outer world images, thoughts, and worries.

Listen without time or place restrictions controlling you.

Be honest and authentic with yourself. If it doesn't feel right, it isn't right.

You can hold onto a thought, relationship, fantasy, place, heirloom, way of viewing a situation, self-loathing, self-pity, feelings from another time, person, or child of origin - if you wish.

But only you can choose to cut the cord, release the ties/patterns that bind and limit your beloved communion with others, who seek to them beings who accept love and soulful bliss.

I am here to tell you, however, that you cannot interpret, perceive, or begin to know the mind or heart of another.

You cannot ask for their heart's desire to come to them, because you do not know if they are ready, or willing to release the blocks to their good, nor, if they are open to receive.

You can pray for them to live honestly.

When one is honest with themselves, they begin the process of release, allow new thought patterns to emerge, fill their hearts, open a space for self-love, and love of another, in preparation for meeting their beloved.

J

9. THE ILLUSION OF FEAR

Dear One,

Blessings to you and your brethren. Today, I speak on the Illusion of Fear.

In your world, if there is one pervasive illusory emotion, it is Fear.

Fear of illness, injury, finances, debt, loneliness, disconnection and fear of one another. Fear thoughts transcend all stages of Earth's form. Minds in fear rely on guidance and ideas generated from Sources that are not of God. There appears to be a pervasive "separateness," insuring one's competitive place, above another, to advance an Earthly goal.

In your world, this begins in childhood when children are expected to perform at specified levels, or else they are labeled as limited, less capable, or a failure. I called the children to me when I walked the Earth to demonstrate The Father's Love.

This categorizing of beings discounts the soul's worth, which is established by GOD. Souls are not separate from other souls, as Oneness comes from The Creator of All.

Fear is ego's hold on generations of humankind, faced with evaluation of worth based on how they measure up to others, in appearance, performance, physical form, wealth, possessions, academic attainment (degrees/awards), and now, algorithms to measure barometers of success.

The constant barrage of worldly mile-markers pushes the ego (mind/body) to achieve more and more, and the mind in human form spirals into low consciousness states, not knowing how to right themselves.

Fear produces anxiety, guilt, and stress, even among the young and those deemed successful by the mile-marker achievements awarded in your world.

Yet, souls cry out for release. This often comes by their own hand, when they believe that the only way to alleviate guilt, fear, and pain of the heart, is by suicide.

I come to you today to remind you, dear one, that there is nothing to fear – (ACIM Lesson 48). You are so worthy, loved, and amazing. How could you not be? You are created by The Divine!

Stop, quiet yourself in any place you come to be. REST with me for 2-5 minutes.
Breathe. Exhale.
Breathe. Exhale.

Does your heart, beat, because of your abilities?
Do your eyes blink under your control?
Feel the peace of PAUSE.
Sink into that. The rest will work out.

Refrain from rash decisions or impulsive acts.
You can have Peace instead of the manufactured angst you bring upon yourself.

Reboot your mind, even for 5 minutes. Practice PAUSE.

In the Silence, you are Loved.

In the Silence, you are Peaceful.

Your Soul recognizes The Spirit of The One Who Knows no fear, only peace.

Pause and Be Still. Be Peaceful.

J

10. TREASURE

Dear One,

Today, I come to speak to you on Treasure. What treasures or keepsakes do you value? Why does one spend time in their world acquiring things that accumulate in their spaces, places, or residences?

The "treasure" of materiality encumbers one's surroundings and the ego mind. The constant clutter of things clutters the mind.

The treasures of materiality in form offer a poor substitute for thoughtful contemplations and the practice of simplicity.

The accumulation of treasure is a diversion from Spirit's purpose. There is no need for adornment or ritualistic ornaments to practice communing with The Divine in peace and stillness.

The quest for treasure has been used to acquire resources from the poor for centuries. Today I tell you, that was never the purpose of my work on Earth's plane.

My work from The Father was ordained and predetermined and I chose to do it. There was always the work – to spread the message of Love (one another as I have loved you), as The Father (loves you), the reason for my being's incarnation into Form.

"Treasure" is not a reward by The Father extended to certain groups of people. The Father's way is not paved with gold, jewels, or property. All worldly goods are creations of the ego. There are no "chosen ones" who The Father deems as worthier. Nor are ones chosen to have an "easy" or coronated incarnation. Those illusions are man-made and have no reality in Truth.

I lived among those whose toils never offered a substantive return. One's work is not an indication of one's worth – merely a means to live in the world.

All ego desires further 'separateness' among His creations.

If one's talents and toils are not serving the greater good, God's purpose, to love and care for all his children - than there is no heavenly value, only a pretense and grand illusion created by ego mind.

As I say in A Course in Miracles, *"Your worth is established by God."*

Your worldly treasure is not lasting – but the love of the Father is eternal. And so, I leave you today to contemplate these words that I impart with the utmost loving heart.

Amen, Amen.

J

11. YOUR LIFE IS YOUR LIFE

Dear One,

You are making your work, your life. That is not truly what The Divine expects of you. Your work is not your life. Your life is your life, and it's yours to live.

There is no job, relationship, or goal that serves your purpose for good unless your mind/spirit connection is activated – and you know it is when your heart feels light.

You are not responsible for changing the world, being a social activist, reworking institutions, or bearing the weight of others on your shoulders.

You are not asked by the Spirit to perform, succeed, show your talents, or compete with others, whether colleagues, family, or strangers.

Each being on Earth goes forward with their soul into the world of form. Each being assumes a body and a personality that is on Earth's plane to learn lessons, impart gifts, and use talents to heal, teach, grow, create, and care.

When detached from expectations, you pursue your purpose-filled calling. When you feel light and joyful, you operate from the zone of Spirit's Inspiration, expressed in form. The God-given talents designed specifically for you, extend to all you encounter.

Some beings (you are one) are here for the purpose of lighting the way for all to recognize their worth, as a child of God, who is loved beyond measure. You know your Source.

You know that your worth is defined by God, not by man's accounting or value system. You know when a 'holy instant' occurs in your work and daily encounters as you feel on-purpose.

But the minute you allow yourself to become entangled in the actions of the world, and those in it, you burden your spirit and cultivate a mind, that is not merely split, but detached from your one true self.

Do not concern yourself with matters that you cannot control, to the exclusion of all other pursuits.

We have it covered and support you. Let go and release it all to our care. We cannot help if our clear guidance is blocked by ego mind's constant thinking and directing your actions.

It's all OK. Mind concerns will cease to be an issue. If you Allow, Spirit will Guide.

Relax and experience more joy.
Smile more.

Breathe deeply.
Find happiness in small and natural pleasures.

Leave matters for Source to handle.

You will know what to say and do.

Spirit is always here to guide, uplift, and support.

J

12. MINDLESSNESS

Dear One,

When your ego state of mind creates a dark mood, you can ask Spirit's Guidance to move you out of a self-perpetuated abyss.

Earth's plane noise does not uplift, calm, or inspire peace and love. Keeping up with "breaking news" is breaking your heart and spirit.

Rather than seeking uplifting soul connections with others, you succumb to streams of unfiltered messages that lower your vibration, resulting in decisions and actions that manifest in emotional or physical pain.

Mindlessness spins out-of-control from one day to the next, and you feel swept into a frenzy whose outcome is neither loving nor joyful. How do you stop the spiral? Ignore signals from the world.

Do not expect the outer world - of accountability, depreciation, evidenced- based outcomes, and data to protect your spirit or acknowledge who you really are.

Ask Source to guide you to feel your own strength, power, beauty, and worth.

You will be redirected to align with your soul self and God within, as you gradually feel moved to heal, help, and smile.

Be still and know that I am God ~ know and believe that you are loved and always guided.

Pause, breathe, and pray.

You will feel lighter.
You are beloved, feel into this.

J

13. ONENESS

Dear One,

I wish to speak today of the Oneness of all and how to "see" another fully.

When I walked the Earth's plane, I did not look away. My eyes met the eyes of my brother/sister in physical form. I looked beyond the body to "see" the soul.

When I walked the Earth's plane, I did not view one as a stranger, enemy, beggar, refugee, criminal, leader, person of authority, person of wealth, leper, or blind man. I heard others say these things and categorize beings, but I saw through the eyes of The Father, All That Is, who knows all.

When I touched the physical hand of someone, there was a deep connection – a healing, a manifestation of The Father, a Oneness, a moment of peace – a joyous recognition, that I and my brother/sister are One with the same Father of all.

There is no separation among souls. There is no division in the Mind of God. There is no order of specialness or rank of superiority.

All are loved, and Source 'sees' no distinction in form. There is no race, ethnicity, gender, occupation, size, health, wealth, attainment, religion, geography, or any other attribute that humans use to categorize other beings in form and in turn, evaluate their own worth by worldly standards.

The Divine Light gave me the gifts of demonstration and unfiltered connection to everyone I met.

The Father who sent Me to Earth, to live and learn among all, proclaimed an everlasting message: Be centered in God's love. Follow the call of The Father, as I did. See someone and meet their soul.

J

14. WHY AM I HERE?

Dear One,

Souls on Earth's plane often ask, "Why am I here?"

"Why am I in this geographical place/location when there are many places I could be living in?"

Some feel an urge to move beyond their places of origin and follow their intuitive guidance. One might relocate because of a work assignment, or order to do so (military, company relocation).

In those matters, one doesn't act freely, but allows the course of events to influence their life's "station" at the time. Each move brings about growth to the person and offers soul work/expansion. Life's process and synchronicities always provide lessons. Some choices delay a relationship or the stability of a place.

There are those who move temporarily when they take a vacation, travel, take a detour, volunteer to help those impacted by famine or traumatic events, are placed in a situation (not by choice), or meet strangers who teach them a lesson that deepens their soul's purpose. One is always learning and can never predict who will be the teacher or the pupil. For soul's work, it matters not where you are physically located.

God is always with you.

J

15. POSSIBILITY

Dear One,

I have come to be with you today to speak on possibility.

Possibility is believing in The Divine in You rather than imitation or depravity.

Open yourself up to greater possibilities and greatness that emanates from your connection to THE DIVINE, who knows no limits. Therefore, all things are possible for you, and nothing constrains you - except your own mind's limitations.
No parameters, fences, boxes, compartments, or restrictions are placed by God.

Therefore, I tell you, open your mind first to all. Do not limit yourself or what you set out to do through the eyes of one in the world of form.
Decide today to create a meaningful visualization of RELEASE.

Shake out the old ideas and beliefs of life. Release, as if you are a free bird who flies about and never questions, as all is taken care of.

The bird has no restrictions on what it can do and has the freedom to explore, try new things, and be open to all there is. When you allow, the SPIRIT guidance opens the vastness of opportunities, discovery, and adventures to you, too. As you RELEASE rigid worldviews of what is POSSIBLE, all things become possible.

Because I am a part of you and you are a part of Me nothing is impossible - for Father/Mother God, all things are possible.

Go forward and live the possible and live your dreams. No limits. Only love today.

Your mind is part of the Mind of God, from which all creation and goodness flows without thought.

And so, you, too, are you. I am with you always. It IS POSSIBLE.

J

16. RESISTANCE AND THE EGO MIND

Dear One,

You may freely choose who you listen and feel connected to, but know that ego is not the Voice of Spirit, nor The Voice that is with you always.

The ego is a personality, body-identified creation of the mind. You have the choice and ability to discount and filter what mind (right or ego mind) you believe or hold onto.

Today is a new day, a good morning as you are alive and have breath in your entire being. Let us talk about this for a moment.

To be truly "alive" means to be open, focused on the now, the moment, the discovery of each experience. The fleeting aspect of life is that it is less than 100 years, which is a reason for you to consider each day as a new day, a blessed day, a time of wonder, and seek the "Holy instant."

It is a sensory experience to appreciate the tastes and textures of a ripened raspberry, view a dragonfly resting on the bougainvillea bush, or notice a hummingbird outside your window hovering in midair.

It is a spiritual experience to sit quietly with eyes closed and ponder nothing.

The Voice of God is heard in stillness with a quiet mind.

You know, peace, calm, and contentment. To be fully alive is an exceptional gift – you have awareness. Your breath and heart are open to stimuli and love. Take in all and give out more than you receive. Do without concern for compensation or form.

Be open to greater possibilities and set no boundaries for the unfolding of your life.
The "you" self is connected to God - Source. Whether your ego mind accepts that or not, it can never be withdrawn or broken.

Today, be the fully alive you in all your intentions – and appreciate yourself.

J

17. FLOW

Dear One,

This day, I come to speak on FLOW.

ALLOW The Holy Spirit to guide you. Create the experiences, people, locales, and situations that expand your Soul's Growth within you. You are here for personal evolution, as a soul in a body with a purpose to fulfill.

You may be back on a path because Spirit has led you to the work, the situation, and the people that you will Divinely impact by your presence and sharing of your gifts. Practice forgiveness, patience, generosity, joy, and reception. Limit thoughts that judge or rationalize.

When you try to figure it out, your ego mind interferes with SOURCE'S FLOW. Flow supports movement and forward action. When you block Flow, you're stuck, bottlenecked, and prevented from your receiving and extending Universal Good.

Change is coming. You have asked to be led to people, opportunities, and situations that support your growth and work on the planet. You will meet higher entities of light.

You play a significant part in God's purposeful plan. Make the conscious choice to:

Go with the Flow

Go where the Flow leads you.

Be in the Flow from Spirit.

Your body will give you positive feedback. Your intuition will be heightened, your heart will be free and light.

Your internal organs will be relaxed. Abundance is part of the flow. Flow stands for:

Freely

Let

Oh my God

Work.

Believe it to be so as you go about your day.

J

18. JUDGMENT

Dear One,

Your mind is still determining right or wrong, and imposing judgment on events, people, situations, and outcomes.

These affect your emotional state. These result in thoughts of negativity, angst, worry, or retaliation. You are either in a state of peace, or disturbance of that peace. You cannot afford to be in that space for too long.

You are cared for. You are accepted. You are welcomed. You are loved. You are a vessel of love, God's Love, and it sustains you. You are a being of light, here to uplift others on the planet.

You will guide, and be guided through, by, and in communion with others. You are being led to experiences and people who will enrich and renew your soul connection to the Holy Spirit.

Your light is energized, not depleted by thoughts of the past, prior mind conditioning, judging yourself, or competing with other beings in form. Let go of all concerns.

Be in a state of wonder, grace, gratitude, and expectation of new experiences.

And so, it is.

J

19. BE OPEN TO LOVE AND LIGHT

Dear One,

You have concerns about situations that do not serve you. You are provided for daily and have your needs met. Your concerns appear to be projections into the future, and these are usually NOT in your control.

But what I can tell you, is to let Spirit handle the things in your mind, and you be in your moment-to-moment light.

The Divine cannot assist you if your mind is befuddled, fueled with fear, or in worry thoughts, because then, it is you who tries to figure things out.

Beings who say they trust Spirit's guidance, really work overtime to try to plan, figure it out, hold onto situations and people who no longer serve their purpose, or contribute to Divine good.

You do not desire lack, so why do you think about it all the time? Relax, let go of the angst, drive, push, list of things to accomplish, and just be in the moment.

Be open to opportunities. Allow good and light energy to flow to you.

Appreciate your gifts from the Universe.

Realize that you, and others, ARE a gift to the Universe.

Smile and be light.

J

20. HEALING ON ONE'S SOUL JOURNEY

Dear One,

Each receives, in one way or another, lessons on their soul journey. A strong body, and an even stronger-willed personality/ego, attempt to control conditions. Each must be still, seek guidance, and clarity. A life's work and value system undergo dramatic shifts when physical and emotional malaise manifest.

One often implores, "Do you think I asked for this?"

If your lesson is acceptance, and you choose to be in control, you will have additional lessons. If your lesson is generosity, you'll have multiple lessons if you do not release your gifts. If you ask and you don't receive, could it be that you do not want to hear the answer?

The power to heal is within the heart and mind. Few realize this truth. When situations warrant immediate and regimented treatment, one will be guided to take-charge practitioners.

When medical determinations appear serious, they are viewed by man, not by God. Beings in form possess an inherent soul connection to Spirit, but prioritize their place in a materialistic world.

Belief and dedication to cultivating one's gifts – and a lightened heart, delimits negativity and allows healing energy to surround the body.

Calming the mind through meditation, stillness, and time in natural spaces, moves one towards inner healing.

Each being is loved and cared for. Receive this love, with grace and gratitude. Accept and believe: "There is no power greater than the God Force within, and I will this to be."

Healing comes from Spirit. Since all human form is finite, we support all souls with love and grace to move forward with peace.

J

21. ROLE-PLAY

Dear One,

All bodies play a role. You have assumed a body to be in form. And through that form and personality, one moves on the planet to do their contracted work.

But the role one plays does not matter in the grand scheme of all that is.

The role of each person on Earth is to return home to the heavenly Creator of All That Is. Source is not concerned with the body, worldly places, or attainment of goods. These shall pass away.

At any time, all can be gone (jobs, home, health, physical features, friends, environments) – all can and will meet an end, as nothing lasts forever. Nothing except the peace, love, and sanctuary that is the Return to Home and God.

The realities in your world now speak to a fear-based, worry-dominated society and social order that minimizes God's Light. Headlines that bask in an artificial light, limelight, or spotlight - are short-lived.

This is not Divine Light that spreads hope and love to the masses.

Your work, to uplift, inspire, and teach others, offers gifts that are not from artificial sources, but bestowed by The One, Source, Creator, Divine who beckons all to spread joy, happiness, and love. There is no other real, everlasting entity and there never will be.

I bless and honor your passion, light, and connection to all the greatness that Spirit-inspired mind is, in you.

And so it is, as it always is.

J

22. DIRECTED

Dear One,

You are where you are directed to live and be at this time. Your life may be altered at a moment's notice, as time is only a passing blot, and we move our energies continuously.

Your energy is one that needs to stay uplifted, as your vibration is one that others have come to depend upon. Your love and open heart impact more people than negative thinking will in any form. There is a benefit to others when you are at peace, calm, and at rest.

Do not get sucked into worldly drama. You are above that and know that love, and not animosity or retaliation, is the answer.

How you conduct yourself is an example to others.

The Earthly version of love, as a physical spark that connects two bodies in form, is not the Love of God that heals minds, hearts, and beings.

The Love of an Eternal Divine Force is one that transcends the world. It is the purest form of the "love one another," that I spoke of when I walked the Earth.

You are a soul in an Earth form. You are worthy, valued, deserving, and known by The Divine One who created all from the purest love.

There is no one among you who walks separate from this Guiding Light, even when ego actions are the cause of pain and suffering.

The Father's Love brings joy to a heart, a smile to a face, and uplifts the soul being within you. You are purposefully in form to learn, experience love, joy, happiness, abundance without limits, conditions, criteria, or acceptance, and share with others.

You and your brothers and sisters are capable of so much more than what limited thinking allows. There is no distinction of beings in Heavenly Wisdom.

Greet people, be positive, and appeal to the sense of self-assuredness in you when God directs you. Release feelings of unworthiness and accept abundant blessings. Pause and still your thoughts.

All of creation absorbs human energy and reacts to the flow of love or its' absence. Allow Heavenly Wisdom to guide your actions.

When you are steadfast in your Truth, no matter what the outside world presents, your soul and heart connect with Divine Love that remains ever present within you. No outside element, person, place, or experience can change God's Love for you. The Almighty does wondrous works through each being in alignment with Source Guidance.

J

23. LOCATION

Dear One,

Let's examine the feelings attributed to "location."

Some feel exhilarated by new experiences and people they encounter. Others long for people they love, or what they view as 'familiar' places.

Others, seemingly 'trapped' in a location by circumstances they view as beyond their control (family obligations), work, duty (serving country, corporation, community), conditions (illness, war), limitation (poverty, suppression, incarceration), are there to learn lessons, exposure to others teaching them in each location.

Sometimes, the deepest growth of your soul occurs when you are placed in situations that ego-mind perceives as ones that should not be experienced.

You do not practice acceptance. You dismiss the opportunity to learn, forgive, or be right where you are.

The location one currently occupies is also a product of the mind.

One can "limit" freedom to choose and experience love, freedom from fear, lack, or disease, by elevating mind from a physical location.

Often one poses scenarios, "Where do you see yourself living?" "Why do you wish to go there? How do you feel once there?"

Consider that if you were supposed to be somewhere, one of two things would happen: Your heart's desire would unlatch the restraint holding you back, and you would just go where you feel enlightened and light, OR...

You would be sent, relocated, or propelled by the Universe to where you are needed to impact others, or for the growth of your soul.

You choose to reside where you are as a creature of habit. Most are fearful of change -whether it be for a job, direction, partner, or life's living arrangements. Stepping forward into the unknown - comes from a lack of trust and dependence upon the security of "the known."

On the other hand, there are those who can "feel" the vibration of a place and know if the energy feels 'light' or 'heavy.' This affects their response to people and themselves.

In this sense, there is something to be said about following your heart, going to where you feel light, and being fully open to your heart's desire.

When I walked the Earth, after communion with The Father, I went about the work, not moved by worldly emotions, outer circumstances, or a connection to a place.

When you ask for guidance, allow the signs and messages to be. Be still and in the silence ask, "What is this? How does it feel?"

You will receive clarity and direction. It can and does come to you when you are ready.

Heavenly beings know all and see all.

We are aware when you say you're ready, but are not.

We are aware of your soul purpose, but not your ego mind.

Source knows the lessons/experiences that benefit your soul journey.

If you have attended to the lessons that Father/Mother God has placed before you, a new location, experience, connection, and soul being will present at the time designed for you.

J

24. EGO-DEVOTION

Dear One,

I will speak today about Devotion. Devotion is often linked to ego beliefs and infers a level of sacrifice. One gives up their self to attend to another, pursue an ambition, support a cause, or align with a focused goal. Devotion has characteristically been deemed as a worthy phenomenon.

If the focus is genuine, authentic, heartfelt, and purposeful, one feels at peace with their service/efforts. Others consider devotion as self-validation of one's "mission" in life.

Devotion often accompanies giving up self, in service to, or in value of another, or ego-based cause, rather than acting on Source-inspired guidance.

While appearing honorable, devotion often overtakes the life of the individual devoted to a cause, passion, person, or project. Ego Devotion seeks external validation. One informs others of their sacrifice and service, for personal gain, sympathy, or notoriety.

Spirit-guided "holy instants" offer opportunities for two or more souls to convene to usher in love, inner peace, calm, comfort, or compassion. Ego Devotion initiates an individual into a select group, working for a cause or outcome. This dedication consumes one's personhood.

Ego Devotion creates an unnatural state that brews resentment and discontent. During instances when the work, creation, or dedication to another becomes burdensome, one experiences an emotional imbalance in physical form and mind.

Ego Devotion attempts to control the external, under the guise of martyrdom, victim, or selfless supporter.

Ego Devotion assumes a false purpose, when the giver feels that they are sacrificing their own life to care, work, or serve.

Ego Devotion performs service with the intention of securing favor or reward in the future.

Ego-Devotion seeks compensation. The giver determines that a settling of sorts is due to them. These mind-based ideas align with a worldly thought system that maintains accounts: who and how one is rewarded for their efforts.

Devotion to externals is always a directed focus to not deal with 'self,' but a place/being/task outside the self, as one's reason for living.

By heeding the ego voice within, one is directed to a duty that can sidetrack, postpone, or even remove one from their soul's path in this lifetime. A misalignment of purpose instigates and harbors contrary emotions that fester under the surface of a form's outward exterior.

One may demonstrate anger, resentment, and entitlement when devotion is contrived.

Ego Devotion justifies one feeling put upon, inconvenienced, taken advantage of, mistreated, used, or suffering a physical, personal, or worldly loss.

Be mindful of devotion that contributes to loss of self (attention, time, care, purpose, joy), as the task becomes the absolute focus of one's life.

All devotion, whether to one's child, aging parent, partner, brother/sister in arms, or community, requires balance.

When devotion is Divinely designed for soul growth, action feels purposeful and emanates from love.

When one is in alignment to Spirit's purpose, they are outwardly engaged, genuinely authentic and display acts of love, joy, care, compassion, and dedication to others.

When doing The Father's work on Earth, ego-direction interactions are replaced by a soul's connection to Source, as every interaction extends boundless goodness.

J

25. EGO DEVOTION IN SPECIAL RELATIONSHIPS

Dear One,

Let us continue. Ego Devotion relationships encumber beings, as they are often unbalanced and, at times, dysfunctional.

For these reasons, special relationships within couples, families, schools, communities, organizations, and institutions assume a mental, emotional, physical, or geographical toll that might be viewed as bondage, where one's ego-self surrenders to the will, whim, and mood of others.

Low-level emotions (resentment, guilt, disdain) often accompany day-to-day functions in compromised life interactions, where one is not free to give authentically, from a place of love. The expectation to be devoted, is often viewed as an imposition.

This is not a holy or Blessed relationship.

Beings seek to escape, either through substances, addictions, distractions, or avoidance tasks. These behaviors postpone addressing the underlying identification. One feels unworthy or devalued, and fails to honestly state that they are not at peace with the situation they are placed in.

Each being is either purposefully aligned or resisting. The soul self longs to feel the grace of God without strings, attachments, or any type of pressure to do, be, or act in any form.

The spirit of each soul needs to thrive, flourish, and grow on their path and journey of grace, joy, and purposeful experiences.

Dwell on this and know that acceptance or rightful action will fill your being and soothe a prodded, push-pulled heart to counter the effects of ego devotion – an unattainable, man-made goal.

Go forth in love and peace today and be filled with Spirit's love and light.

J

26. BOUNDLESS LOVE

Dear One,

There are many levels of relationships. People are brought together to accomplish something. Romantic love, infatuation, and physicality - the stuff of mythology, media, movies, music, and materialism, are of ego mind.

Romantic love is often the greatest illusion. The beginning of any relationship is a belief, a fabrication, a Hollywood scene, with attention, expressions of care, and concern based upon an ideal of what love feels like when 'love' is confused with infatuation.

The radiance of lovers observed by all is just a flicker of the Love from God to you. The Love of God embraces the now, the present, and the forever because it is boundless. Boundless love knows no starting or ending point. Boundless love is not marked by an anniversary or a date.

Human beings ask for peace but bring disharmony into some of their closest relationships (mates, family, co-workers). They seek reasons to be separate. Instead of loving the person in the moment, in the now, they find fault with the result, the absence of love, the absence of connection.

This is not the way to peace for anyone. You look for external sources to bring joy and happiness.

Boundless love has no boundaries that stipulate, "This is mine; that is yours," nor is there an accounting or expectation that delineates, 'What I do for you; or what you do for me."

Boundless Love can never be extinguished, does not look for excuses to change its dedication, commitment, or actions and is constant and sustaining.

Ask the Holy Spirit to enter your relationships. View each person with the eyes of love. Engage in a state of mutual appreciation, moment by moment. Radiate love through your smile, touch, essence. You are here to love and love fully.

Be light, knowing that as you radiate your love, the fullness of love's miracles come to you and all you encounter.

J

27. TRUTH AND BOUNDARIES

Dear One,

There is no time in Universal Mind.
All that IS – is. There are no restrictions or expectations from me or Spirit, as this is an Earthly construct that doesn't exist in TRUTH.

In Truth, we are all on the same path to the One. In Truth, there is no need to be somebody because your soul IS, and that is.

The world, as you perceive it, is limited and fragmented. Separateness is the way that one's personality-being remains apart from another.
The notion of Boundaries that need to be protected or defined comes from a fear-based mind.

But that is not your natural state. When you rest in your natural state of God's mind, you feel peace instead of fear, grace instead of conflict, and a holy purpose brings togetherness that soothes any worldly hurt.

There is no space for both love and hate or fear and trust to co-exist in the mind of a child of God. You, my sisters and brothers, are offered total harmony with your soul self, if you focus on a singular force of good to be with you always.

Love is your natural state. You do not need to accept your natural state or embrace it – because it is an ever-present glow that is never extinguished, try as you may. You will Return to the love that created you. The Love of God is beyond human thought. The Love of God has no substitute on Earth's plane nor in the universe.

The Love of God exists in the souls of all beings, and as such, the Way of Love is to follow signaling from within.

When I said, "Come Follow Me," it was not a call to prayer or supplication. It was instead, a call to affirm the presence of Love in action.

Following The Way is clear and on purpose. The purpose, for me, was to never become distracted by the world.

The direction from The Father kept me on purpose, as I had no doubt that my work was a natural extension of Love.

How can Love direct us, you may ask?
Love creates all, as it is the only forever disposition of the true self. Truth is the way of The Father, who is constant in His Love. The Father loves, The Father is.
Nothing else that you focus on, with such intent, is real or lasting. For me, my dear ones, it was simple to always...

Walk in love, See in love, Speak in love, And be in love. Truth is. Love is. Return to the Truth of your Soul Self.

Truth will set you and (your mind) free.

J

28. OUTCOMES

My Dear One,

You appear anxious and downtrodden. But why?

Do not permit these feelings to be prolonged in your mind. Check in with your emotions.

Angst, frustration, disappointment, impatience, assertiveness, whining, lamenting, and frustration are not higher frequency energies.

These perpetuate and replicate other lower energies that send beings into a tailspin of doubt, negativity, and blame.

Outcomes are not determined by the mind, as are algorithms prepared by models or artificial intelligence.

When one tries to control outcomes, hold fixed expectations, or a firm desire, mind sets you up for disappointment.

A fixed outcome is never a sure thing, as there is no formula for predictability in your world.

What you think will happen is a sign that you persist in managing your life according to the world and not the Divine Life within.

You worry and concern yourself with externals that you have no control over. This limits your good because you cannot fathom what The Creator may have in store for you.

Tap into your internal Divine Intelligence.

Breathe (3x) to defuse the aura of scarcity, lack, and patterns of helplessness.

Breathe in the Light, The Abundance of Creativity, and the Love that surrounds you.

You are a child of God, and God is Unlimited, Abundant Love, whose Guidance is a presence to be affirmed, by stating:

I TRUST.
I AM BLESSED.
I ALLOW.

You do not know when, where, or how a connection will be forthcoming to move you forward on a path that you have never considered in your limited belief system.

Unexpected inspiration, human ingenuity, and creative expression in form are signs that Spirit is working in your life and the lives of all souls in Earth form, as always.

Be Present, Be Open.

Feel into the awareness of what positive thinking is.
Create the Life you experience at this moment.

Go now and enjoy the Synchronicity that awaits!

You are loved and cared for.

J

29. REST IN ME

Dear One,

I come to you this day with abundant love and blessings. Put all thoughts out of your mind. Turn over yourself – your true self – to my Guidance.

Consider this time devoted to opening to the Peace and comfort that I offer to uplift your Spirit this day.

How may I guide you to feel a bit lighter?
How may I relieve the burdens that plague your mind and manifest as "real" to you?

The concerns you have fade away when you consider that your True Self is guided by a loving, comforting Presence that does not ask for anything, demand a task be done, or expect something in return.

Love Is - it always is. The Presence guides, comforts, offers peace, and is a constant Source of Love. You can choose to be in the Presence.

When you align with your breath, your mind quiets, and the focus is on nothing, you are held in my embrace.

You are cradled in the arms of a Loving God who knows that your Soul is a manifestation of the same Spirit touched by the Divine.

There is nothing else for you to do... Hand "life" as you experience form over to me. I'll bring you Rest.

When I said, "Rest in Me," I meant Rest in Spirit – the respite from distractions of the world. These attach to you through ego mind.

Your constant state of "thinking," considering options, and planning the future, blocks Guidance from me and the All That Is. The "rest" is you laying all things of this world aside.

Nothing in this world is real, permanent, lasting.

Why do these matters that are so transient hold so much power over you, that your entire being responds to triggering world views that manifest outwardly as fear, guilt, hurt, insecurity, anxiety, doubt, remorse, or inadequacy?

These are never signals from Source. These are, however, signs that you are listening to the world that is separate from Source.

My Way Is the way of the Father.
My Way leads you home to Love.
My Way offers Comfort.
My Way brings you Peace.

I am always here for you, and my Love is always a constant refuge from the distractions of the world. To be in the world, but not of it, takes discipline.

To choose, in every instant, how you will transcend concerns to be fully present, knowing that you were placed in a body to do "good in your capacity to do so" does not equate to acquiring 'goods.'

Doing good is guided by Source. Follow the guidance of the Spirit as you go about your day in alignment with God's purpose for you. The pause you take to reconnect with Spirit moves you forward.

Ask, as did I, "What shall you have Me do?" This is a prayer to Source for guidance, and with Guidance, nothing is impossible.

Go now and spread this message. Amen, Amen.

J

30. DISCONTENT AND CRIPPLED SPIRIT

Dear One,

To stay above the fray means to walk in the light. To adapt the way of the Masters who demonstrated deep faith and trust as they transcended the toils of daily life and tribulations.

What separates those who manage their emotions and mind energies from those pressed down by the weight of the world?

The peace from within offers a resource and pillar of strength given to all without privilege. Acceptance of what is, is always your choice.

Each being possesses the free will to accept and peacefully reconcile in mind situations one is faced with in the present. To do otherwise creates discontent, which if prolonged, breeds dis-ease – the physical manifestation of discontent with one's circumstance.

Discontent is an outward toll on one's spirit that manifests in the human form.

Discontent stems from ego thinking and low-level emotions that are not reconciled. Mind internalizes these beliefs. Anxiety, tension, fear, envy, and comparison manifests as deep emotional malaise that cripples one's spirit.

A crippled spirit can be a greater block to inner peace than any physical malady.

A crippled spirit causes prolonged, persistent physical ailments, and disease, often referred to in your world as terminal, degenerative, or chronic conditions. The ability to overcome these conditions of the body requires a spiritual solution. One's Spirit must move through emotions that constrict Divine Love and Light.

Shift mind thinking from limitation: I lack. I am alone. I am weak. I am limited. I am not loveable. I cannot do this.

To affirmation: I walk with Spirit. Divine Love fills my being. Divine opportunities abound. I am abundantly blessed. I am strong with God. I am so loved. With God, all things are possible.

Your connection to Source/Spirit is eternal. The body may feel pain but is never separated from Presence.

When one intuits un-ease and holds fast to lower-level beliefs, they remain stuck in mind's dominant message to self. Seek out other beings who see the light in you. Feel into the EASE of Spirit. Jumpstart your Soul Self.

Proclaim:
I AM A CHILD OF THE DIVINE.
I AM BLESSED BEYOND MEASURE. I AM JOYFUL.
Believe this to be true.
And so it is.

J

31. RADIANT LOVE

Dear One,

Today, I speak to you of Love. Radiant love, no matter what, embraces you. Sink into that feeling.

You ask for a Holy Relationship. You will be aware of the twin flame seeking your union, and you will both advance the mission of "The ONE." All of us want love. But what do we do to ourselves when we act unloving, mean-spirited, or in a self-critical, one-ups-man-ship manner?

If you talk love... it's just talk.

If you act loving on some days, but not on others, uncertainty colors your actions. What is the next 'emotion'? Others cannot predict...Will you extend love or fear?

How is it that 'loving' people hold grudges, plan retaliation, and act in ways that are personally and collectively destructive? If you withhold love for any reason, you erode trust and separateness runs as deep as a crater-like chasm.

Love of yourself is required to love another.
Love recognition is required to love fully.
Love expression is required to generate a singular flow of energy that moves from one to the other in a state of mutual appreciation, moment by moment.

Be an example of living, growing, and abundant love.

Ignite the love.

Radiate love through your smile, touch, essence.

You are here to love from your Soul-being.

Be light. Know that as you radiate your love, Love's miracles and fullness come to you and all you encounter. Open your heart to love… smile and be happy.

J

32. TRUTH

Dear One,

There is only Truth. Truth never changes.
You are loved. You are light.
You are a child of the Divine.
Therefore, you are Divine.
You are not your body.
You are not your human thoughts.

At any time, change course, accept the TRUE story to replace the one that took hold of you. Freewill might not physically liberate a prisoner, but confining principles in an uncontrolled mind that believes ego thoughts, manifests as physical and emotional maladies.

To this end, one must step out from habits of mind, artificial noise, and worldly influences that are unbalanced. Be open to the communion of the Creator's Truth.

The soul yearns to connect with other souls.
How can you benefit yourself if you're only with yourself?
You hear, see, and think only what your mind wants to hear, see, and think, which limits new perceptions. This is the prevalent disease of your world.

Face-to-face human interactions that are genuine and authentic must replace solitary self-confinement. Living in community supports common goals and uplifts hearts. Seek out groups, commune with others, and make a choice for the growth of your soul.

But first, guard your mind that may have been closed to Divine Guidance.

Refresh and exhale all that no longer serves the Christ-mind in your heart. The choice to start anew is always present.

Go with peace and love.

J

33. CONDITIONS

Dear One,

I will speak upon conditions that appear as 'real' in form. Pain, malaise, or illness in physical form are not recognized in the Mind of God. There is no sickness. All are perfect, healed, and loved.

The Divine does not assign conditions or dualities such as sickness/health or wealth/poverty. All are connected to Source in all ways. In the beyond, the body's conditions are transcended.

Your words – even words said to yourself when no one hears – have potentials to heal or bind. Inner thoughts are spontaneous, and the slightest negativity in mind, affects your physical being. When one manifests a condition, there is an underlying belief held so firmly by one's thought system, that reinforces fear, anxiety, or unworthiness.

What is manifested is in sync with belief. Many in your world state, "God must be punishing me." God is love and does not send conditions or plagues upon humanity.

When one projects worry or perceives a certain outcome, fear is mind's go-to response. The outer is a mirror of the inner. When one is on purpose, grateful, appreciative, and full of loving thoughts, their physical form manifests contentment.

Spirit does not provide a specific diagnosis for physical ailments or conditions, because it is not real or present in Truth.

What is the purpose of your present condition for your soul's development? Can you release this condition, or is it something that you choose to hold onto? Remember, God a Loving Father, does not send illness nor its' healing.

Do not pray for a physical miracle. Ask instead for healing of the mind that remains stuck in a particular pattern. If you present with the condition, it is yours to release.

You can Heal yourself when you are living in and on Purpose. You will find that it all works out with no effort on your part.

J

34. IS-NESS OF BEING

Dear One,

Transitions, change, and endings are elements of life on Earth. Situations arise for us to pause, appreciate, and accept what the pace of life, if not guarded, brings with it: pressures that impact how one goes about living. Ceremonies become place-keepers for life's journey. Beings do not savor the experiences of aliveness. Hurried breath is not cleansing nor peaceful.

Rather, deep, stressful exhales indicate frustrations and challenges. Step away, step back, silence the noise/news/messaging.

Simplicity is healing. Each of our senses becomes an instrument for presence. To be present in the isness of being happens across the Earth's plane when one takes time to just be still. The present moment is. The interaction is. The breath is. The hummingbird seeking nectar is. Acknowledge the interwoven being-ness of how you feel in each instant.

Is-ness is not next-ness nor was-ness.

There is only present-ness, and it liberates us from any plan, preparation, or to-do list. Is-ness soothes the mind and offers awareness of the is-self in every moment- a gift from The Divine when unexpected miracles occur.

IS is Presence.

J

35. MESSENGERS OF THE SOURCE OF LOVE

Dear One,

Beings are we all. Blessed by the love of The Divine, the peace of the Christ, the love of The Father. I possess no divinity that is worthy of homage or adoration.

I am one – the same with all. None deserves idolization.

The notion of saints and statues to mark the life on earth of another being is insane – ludicrous. The lives of ordinary beings doing 'extraordinary things' are evidence of one's tapping into Divine Order of the Universe that runs through all.

There is no hierarchy of purpose because all are beings from the same One that guides us all. To consider this as supernatural or worthy of adoration, is misplaced attention. Any being connected to Source can move mountains, lead movements, or do what appears to be impossible. As I transcended my body, so too, can you transcend concerns of this world.

Live in the world with this knowledge. Call on the Holy Spirit. Ask for clarity, direction, and purpose. Believe in the response provided by messengers of the Source of Love. Be open to Divine Guidance. Choose to listen to the Guidance.

You are not alone in figuring out life.

Sense intuitively when you are suddenly placed in a situation, face a condition, or experience a circumstance and allow healing that is beyond your own means of orchestration.

"Ask, and you shall receive," connects you to Source. In stillness you can hear God's Message. Receiving offers the way forward. in world view, receiving is demonstration for goods, relationships, or livelihood. It is a tangible.

But The Source of Love extends love, grace, compassion.

You and all are placed here as beings ~ messengers of The Source of Love. Each messenger extends God's love across humanity, in every experience, in every instant, when you are in touch with The Oneness within.

Ask often, ask with an open heart and mind, trust fully, and you shall receive.

J

36. DIRECTION FROM SPIRIT

Dear One,

How does one know when God directs them? Direction from Spirit occurs quickly. The message is simple. There's a feeling in your heart that this is yours to do.

How does one know it's the right thing to do?

Something shows up when the timing is part of God's timing for you, your purpose, and your soul's growth on the Earth's plane. Sometimes, Spirit's Direction includes a change.

The change is not always something your ego self wants to embark upon. Ego-mind wants to know details, outcomes, and all the what-ifs, answered.

Spirit doesn't deal with 'what ifs.'

It is present, and KNOWS what will bring your highest growth. Spirit sees the whole picture; you see only a slice.
Spirit knows that some level of discomfort in your mind, body, and intuition ushers in a new level of awareness, that shifts habits of mind and form. You can ignore or postpone heeding direction from Spirit. You have a choice and free will.

When you are aligned with Spirit, your work comes to you naturally. You uplift others with your presence, skills, and shared experience.

Spirit works through you, bringing joy, love, peace, and support during a moment when you feel an authentic connection with another. This is how the body is useful.

The body does not exist forever. A limited time is offered for each being to finish out its time in physical human form on Earth. Yet the soul remains, is constant, is part of God, and will move on to its place in the Spirit realm.

J

37. RISE ABOVE

Dear One,

The Divine in you goes with you always. The Earth world is not your home, no matter where you lay your body down – home is not a place or a locale. It is not possible to be truly at home on Earth's plane.

Your home is a Divine Presence filled with love. Know that you, and all, are part of The Divine Presence of God, The One, Creator.

You live within the Earth's body, but the ego is strong, calculating, and divisive. If the ego went away – the Oneness of All would bring only Oneness to the planet.

It seems that in these times, you and all Earthly dwellers are, in Earth terms, directed by "ego" wants, desires, staging, and actions that are finite.

These outward presentations of form separate beings, based upon categories that are inventions of human mind.

God is not judgmental. Spirit does not know age, physical attributes, conditions, cultures, or circumstances.

When I walked the Earth, my dear one, there were ego divisions meant to separate beings: slave/master, conquered/conqueror, powerless/powerful, leper/clean.

While I lived among you, I was aware of corruption, anger, fear, compliance to the will of the ruling body (Emperor King), and how edicts of the powerful ruled the everyday life of my peers.

But these were not configurations that I dwelt upon.

These human conditions are not of God, divined by God, or systems that The Father of All has an awareness of – for these are not part of the Mind of God.

See nothing as real. Accept what is of God, from whom all that is real emanates. Judge not your being, nor any others, by Earthly standards.

For what is in form, holds neither permanence, nor power.

The God Mind emanates love, compassion, care, and is separate from lower-level energies of fear, competition, jealousy, hate, gossip, retaliation, and a host of emotions that contribute to physical manifestations (in body) that erode the Oneness of The Father.

Lightworkers on your planet are reminded to hold the light, channel the love, speak uplifting words, and keep the mind clear of negative vibrations that pollute one's environment, more so than any toxic substance.

During these days, when souls are often the only beacon of light, do not succumb to the pervasive energy of your time.

Instead, act as if I, Jeshua, the Sonship, and your brother, guide your spirit, hold your hand, walk along with you, and act as a buffer between ego thoughts and The Divine Source of real and everlasting GOOD - the essence of your Soul self.

See nothing as real except what is from God.
Rise above chatter.
Rise above world energy.
Rise above divisive messaging. RISE

J

38. DIS-EASE

Dear One,

I send love and light to you on your path to The Father.
The Earth's plane and all other dimensions are Soul Schools.

You live, learn, develop, and share your gifts in alignment with your purpose until you return to Source.

Learning in human form presents ego/body challenges.

The world's influences inculcate habits that reinforce negativity, encourage gossip, comparison of beings, and constant stimulation that prompts ego reactions. A mind that replays dominant worldly messages to self, is stuck and emotionally hurting.

When one cannot feel relief from negative thinking, one experiences Dis-ease. Dis-ease plagues human form.

Dis-ease presents as a deep emotional malaise that cripples one's spirit. Dis-ease binds the ego mind to painful thoughts and self-perceptions.
Dis-ease manifests in physical form after prolonged inner discontent. Dis-ease assumes chronic conditions due to the mind's refusal to accept what is.

Dis-ease strengthens when the mind attempts to negotiate with what is.

All beings have free will. At any time, you can change course or consider a new story to replace ego thoughts that have taken hold of you.

Free will might not physically liberate a prisoner, but an uncontrolled mind, bound by dis-ease, fails to experience the peace, love, and joy of The Divine.

Accept, peacefully reconcile, and release situations that disturb your peace. To do otherwise, only perpetuates discontent and dis-ease.

Live in community. Support others through compassionate service.

Offer a smile and kindness even when experiencing pain in form. One's mind, which may have been closed to possibilities for too long, needs to open to Source's light within.

Make the inner change with the outer. To this end, one must create peace from within, which is the resource and pillar of strength given to all without privilege.

The soul yearns to connect with other souls.

Commune with others, make a choice for the growth of your soul. Genuine and authentic face-to-face human interactions, heal, as the mind focuses on the 'holy instant.'

The body deteriorates, but the connection to Source is constant. The body feels pain but cannot be separated from the Flow of Spirit's Light.

The mind feels pain when separation thoughts prevail.

There is only Truth. Truth never changes.

You are loved. You are light. You are a child of the Divine. You are Divine. You are not your body. You are not your thoughts.

Choose again – think without limits.

J

39. PEACE

Dear One,

The collective beings of the world seek peace. They ask in prayer for peace. They have no use for hostilities, war, violent acts, or mass destruction. They seek peace. They seek calm.

Where are the peacemakers among you?

As in my day, do not look to the powerful or the leaders of nations. They succumb to a worldly quest for dominion over living creatures. They allow others to weave a path of destruction and suffering, effecting plant, animal, and human forms.

What you see and acknowledge in the outer world is temporary, as is your time on Earth.

Chaos cannot serve you or the world for long. Your being feels uprooted like a massive cedar unearthed in a storm.

If you come from a place of peace within, your being offers harmoniousness to all around you. You are anchored, knowing that "The One" who sent you will direct you.

Inner peace offers a refuge from the busyness of mind, chatter, and personal expectations. The inner controls (effects) the outer.

Inner peace comes from knowing that the God in you, is in others. Your mind shifts from outer concerns to the inner consciousness of Spirit.

When you are in the midst of internal turmoil, your outer world does not manifest peace. This duality within your being disturbs your peace.

When you say you believe, but negotiate with God when called to do the work, your heart is torn, and your mind is split.

Surrendering to the Holy Spirit means, that you turn over your cares, worries, work, and thoughts, and are open to Spirit's guidance in each moment. You align mind from split, to affirming God's purpose for you.

Yes, you are in the world of form, but Source goes there with you. There is no reason for emptiness when Spirit extends love.

Find the connection to your inner harmony.
Be STILL.
Take a few minutes to rebalance your being.
Connect to the God Force within you.
In the silence, contemplate what brings lasting inner peace.
You feel what does *not* yield this: illusions, drama, or false attachments. To be fully free, one must cultivate inner peace.

Find time for peace and stillness of mind.
Contemplation time is not wasted. It offers a pathway from which one can hear and recognize Messages from Source.

J

40. REMINDER

Dear One,

You do not know what's best for your growth on Earth's plane. Your path is one that will be directed if you do not resist.

Be flexible as something/someone may be placed in your path to move you, not only forward in your thinking, but in a new direction/situation/ location.

Prepare for new opportunities and people in your life. Be open to direction from Source.

The living breathing Spirit knows your heart, and your heart is Love. When the mind succumbs to fear thoughts or what's-next thinking, lower energy thoughts take hold, and you project beliefs of the world. You are not your body. You are not your thoughts.

Exhale the concerns you have, even for a moment. Redirect your mind and be in the stillness.

In stillness, your being is calm, still, and restored.

Take the Peace of God with you. Keep the Peace of God in Mind. Know the Peace of God in your Heart.

There is only Truth. Truth never changes. You are loved. You are light. You are a child of the Divine. You are Divine.
That is all.

J

41. DOUBT

Dear One,

I speak today about matters of mind. Fear-based thoughts consume minds across Earth's plane.

Free will offers freedom to choose.

Humans, drawn to free-wheeling adventures, volunteer their minds for a free-fall plunge into darkness, despair, and DOUBT.

Doubt seeps into minds that believe the world's thought system.
Doubt stymies purposeful action.
Doubt does not cast out fear.
Doubt does not perform miracles in God's Name.
Doubt perpetuates thoughts of inadequacy and reliance on self.

Ask, "Father, how may I learn the lesson of believing?"

Be open. Spirit will fill you up in ways beyond Earthly mind imagining.
Be grateful and expectant.
Do not doubt for an earth second. It is not your doing, anyway.
Trust Spirit's timing for your highest and best - to be.
Stay balanced with your breath and heartbeat in the present moment.

Today, accept great love with great faith.

Breathe, Breathe, Breathe.

Inhale Love. Exhale Doubt.

Your angels will make way the way.

And so, it Is.

Trust.

J

42. FAITH, TRUST, LOVE

Dear One,

Your world is at a crossroads, poised to make a leap into the unknown, the unchartered, the Universal Beyond. When you say you believe in God but withhold love, your heart is heavy, and your mind is split. The only path forward is through FAITH-TRUST-LOVE. If you do not trust God, who do you TRUST? Do you trust your own mind system to guide you, along with the world's view? It appears so.

The heart that extends LOVE is guided by The Divine. The right mind that demonstrates FAITH in Source follows through on directed action.

Be kind, even in the face of mean-speaking. Be gentle, even in front of brute force. Be calm, even as the outer faces turbulence. Be centered in ME, even when fearful thoughts attempt to shake your core. Be in this moment, the now.

Fall into each experience, affirming, I am grateful. I am loving and generous. I am a living, loving Spirit of the Christ.

Light will shine through to the world. Stay neutral. Display less emotion to outcomes. Know that God loves you. Spirit will orchestrate Guidance for the highest purpose for all.
That is all
J.

43. DECEMBER

Dear One,

The message of Christ is the Call to live in peace, be humble, practice forgiveness, contemplate how God's love manifests in your life, show compassion, do works of charity, aide strangers, feed the hungry, clothe the poor, give thanks to the Father for His Love that transcends time, and be STILL each day.

There is no satisfaction or deep fulfillment that comes from staging re-enactments. The separateness of humanity appears to be a dilemma that cannot be reconciled with fake trees, lights, and frivolous accoutrements displayed prominently in the world of seasonal celebration linked to my material appearance on Earth.

You do not need to wait for a sign from a star.

People need compassion in your world, but few rise to support their plight.

Spirit calls all to heal, bring joy, offer food, shelter, and demonstrate care for each other on this day and all days, wherever you are. Opportunities present for each soul to connect to another with Love and Compassion.

I did The Father's work. I saw each being through the eyes of The Father, who Knows All, and is All That IS.

I was uplifted in Spirit.

Fulfillment comes from heart to heart, soul to soul, eye to eye, meeting of all. That is the way to give during this man-made "season" of giving.

You, too, will be uplifted in Spirit when you act with purpose to bring joy to others through your deeds and dedicated, heartfelt, compassionate acts of giving.

That is all.

J

44. EXPERIENCES

Dear One,

Today, I speak about Experiences. Each body has experiences. These are often judged and determine the value and worth of one's day. Experiences occur frequently, from rise in the morning to rest at night.

How has your day been? Do you offer an accounting of gratitude while meeting your brother with kindness and love, or has judgment or guilt swept into your thoughts?

It takes courage to see the joy in every instant. Present-ness is the state of detaching from the world and the pace of it... to just be present in each experience.

The pace of the world has pushed the limits on the number of experiences that one engages in - almost subconsciously. Pressures associated with time, constrain the individual's opportunity to be present.

A hurriedness permeates and rushes life's experiences. The senses absorb constant stimuli. The age of multitasking requires that one is always doing.

But doing is the opposite of being. The opportunity to be freely present in all experiences is lost, and so, too, is the lesson. How often does one sit and observe nature? A baby delights in grasping their feet.

Can you appreciate the role that feet offers towards movement, freedom, and joy? Feet can jump, dance, walk, kick, stop, wiggle toes, feel sand, and hold the body erect. Every being has the capacity to consider the innate gifts that surround them.

Breathe and appreciate simplicity in experiences.
Dedicate yourself to your "Being." There is no thought, only stillness. There is no recognition of this world. There is only peace.

That is all.

J

45. GOING SOMEWHERE

Dear One,

You ask, "Where am I to go? Who might I go with?" (As if it is up to you to decide and determine such things). Of course, Holy Spirit can make all decisions if you turn your life over, but your ego mind needs to reconcile the habit of constant thinking.

The notion that going somewhere else, or following another's path will make you happy, is an illusion - a mis-thought. Move beyond imprisoning yourself in an earthly role.

It serves you not to compare yourself to an online universe, when it takes your peace away. How might you do the work you love, find the compensation you need, and let go of attachment to any of it, right where you are? Your life flows based upon lessons and Soul Growth that you ask for.

The emptiness or discontent that you feel, may be readying you for new opportunities and new belief patterns. 'Dying to the old' is the way to move forward. However, it is not so influenced by where you are living or working, as by how you perceive purpose in the world. Do you 'see' from the mind's eye or Divine Direction? Are you blinded by concerns impeding the flow of your blessings? You have not lost the connection nor guidance from Source.

Believe, Be Still, and listen to Spirit rather than the mindless mind's interests. What calls to your soul? What gives you joy?

What makes you smile? It will work out. You know this. It always does.

Surrender and be guided. Lift your spirit to the Lord. Truly, there is a way of looking at this differently.

J

46. DO THIS

Dear One,

When you and others on Earth's plane react from causal identities, your response triggers judgment, attack, fear, and anger. Words of the world do not heal, uplift humanity, bring togetherness, or develop a brother/sisterhood of beings.

Your light is needed in the world, your community, and for Divine interactions with souls you meet. Your light instigates the "holy encounter."

I manifested in human form to demonstrate love, forgiveness-in-action, and healing from The Divine Source of ALL.

When I stated, "Do this in remembrance of me," I did not intend for a ritualized ceremony to be re-enacted. How did this gathering, where we came together as a community, become so distorted for centuries?

The phrase meant, Do Good, Do Kindness, Do Forgiveness in Remembrance of the Spirit of God within you.

The essence of "Do this in Remembrance of Me" is simply: Do good in remembrance of The DIVINE GOD.

SPREAD GOD'S LOVE.

That is all,

J

47. CONCERNS

Dear One,

The message today is: Be in the world without encumberments. Dismiss the endless stream of concerns that manifest as mind's worry thoughts.

Concerns are mindless drains on time, purpose, and dedication to your soul's work on Earth. Concerns initiate stimuli directed by one's mind. Mind focuses on the why of each concern, encounter, situation, and injustice, and sets out to address them. You feed each concern, water it, and share with others. Soon it grows and develops into tiered concerns, that range from small stuff to tragedies.

An undisciplined, encumbered mind allows fear thoughts to fester, signaling a lack of faith and trust that the future, your future, is not placed in the hands of God - but your own.

What has your constant focus on concerns, and reliance on your ego self to problem solve, achieved? Are you more peaceful? Joyful? Loving? Full of Grace? I did not anticipate my day's events, nor concern myself with its unfolding.

Be open to signs and messages. Be ready to do what is yours to do. Be in the moment as it arises, and let it go afterward. Draw in new ways of being. Focus on the light. That is all.

J

48. THE WORLD DREAM IN FORM

Dear One,

I wish to speak on the "dream" - a worldly belief that things work out for some and not for all. We do not view time or achievement the way it is viewed on Earth. A soul is eternal in the beyond/ Earth is a finite experience. Your past does not define you, and your future is not known to you.

The mind that recognizes inner thoughts of doubt, fear, or unworthiness may operate from a base of retaliation, remorse, or depressed states.

Often, sickness results. Many who are "ill," however, are not without hope. If you wish to be guided, ask to be guided. If you wish to be healed, ask to be healed.

You are in a body to serve a purpose. Your body is a vehicle for you to learn lessons, offer love, forgiveness, and be a conduit of works designed for you, by The Father – Our Father. To honor the work often requires honoring use of the body to achieve those means.

For example, a worker in the protection field must be able to use his body for the purpose of physical rescue.

The body, of itself, can do nothing. The body acts on mind's instigation, which is why we cannot say the body reacted, assaulted, or offered consolation.

The body, when used for peaceful purposes, follows Holy Spirit's direction. Through Divine Intervention your hands, mind, and heart, heal, offer peace, love, and joy.

This means that the care of the body supports God's plan.

Do you not realize that no matter what form you take on Earth, you will be loved and welcomed when you shed your body and enter The Father's house for eternity?

Hold that thought for 3 minutes and feel a sense of peace, love, wholeness, and love.

J

49. LET IT ALL GO

Dear One,

Why be sad and gloomy? You are alive. Life force flows within you. You can share food with a friend, practice kindness, and heal through your presence, essence, and uplifting words.

Your mind plays games even as you know that the rules, ideas, and belief systems are not from Holy Spirit's Guidance.

You know better, on all levels, especially the spiritual and soul levels.

You know why you are here, and how your being is meant to fulfill your soul's purpose in form, at this moment in Earth time.

You know, "He who sent you will direct you."

You know that as you practice Radical Trust, things fall into place.

Release worries, concerns, fears, untruths, and world's spectacles.

Release concerns, attachments, and outcomes to Holy Spirit.
The highest and best will flow from The Divine, All That Is, to you – the vessel of reception.

Do not dwell on anything but God's love for you.

You will be directed.

Worry will cease to occupy your thinking.

Extend Peace, not turmoil.

Follow guidance from within.

LET IT ALL GO!

That is all.

J

50. FULFILLMENT

Dear One,

Today, I wish to speak on Fulfillment. Things are out of balance. The void in the human heart grows deeper, even in a world where advancements offer a collective collaboration of good works.

Humans quest for more things, experiences, and opportunities. Acquiring stuff overuses resources and depletes human energies and Earth's natural gifts.

Procuring goods, services, land, or personal desires does not satisfy the soul, heal the mind, or nourish the heart that longs for love, joy, and purpose. This Consumption hunger gives rise to a poverty of heart – an absence of authentic joy.

Busying oneself with planned or unplanned activities is not a truly spiritual practice. For many, busyness is the chosen antidote for loneliness. Busyness is distinctly different from purposefulness.

Time devoted to fulfilling your purpose and following The Father's message, not only stills the racing heart and mind, but guides one to fulfillment of one's calling.

Fulfillment comes from serving, leading, caring, healing, creating, and connecting with Spirit's inspired flow. Through your hand, body, and talents, you touch a heart, comfort a being, address a common cause, and uplift humanity at the Spirit level.

The Father endows all with expressive gifts. Life alone is a gift. If you are alive, Our Father has an assignment for you.

As was Truth with all healing attributed to me, The Divine works with, in, and through you, too.

Embrace your magnificent journey to the fulfillment of your purpose. The Divine provides all that you need.

J

51. LOVE IN ACTION

Dear One,

Today, I come to speak of Love in Action. "Love one another as I have loved you," emanates from The Father who created you and me, in Divine likeness. I appeared, like you, in human form and assumed personhood with an assignment, which is the same as yours: Heal, Forgive, Teach, and Love.

I am a Son of God, as are you. The Christ mind is a construct that came to be after I transcended the Earth. It is a version of the Oneness exemplified by my following Holy Spirit's direction to practice Love in Action.

When I said, "Come, follow me," it meant to put aside the ways of the world, accept the call, and act in alignment with The Father. Teach and demonstrate through communion with His Love. This is what we are all called to do.

I relayed this with clarity and seriousness of purpose. No other message has ever come from me other than, "Love one another." That is the message, and it has always been.

I am not The Christ to be emulated, sanctified, glorified, ceremonialized, or exalted in rituals and appropriated for materialistic, philosophical, or ideological gain. The use of my being and name to perpetuate hurt, division, separation, and dominance over centuries is an affront to what the Christ Light means.

God, Our Father, is the essence of Love and Light. All work directed by God manifests as Love in action – eternal and forever.

Love in Action means use your Divine gifts, to demonstrate and act with love in all things.

J

52. RELATIONSHIPS

Dear One,

Your heart's desire can come true at any moment if you are direct and honest with yourself. What do you really want? Why do you really want this? How can you achieve this outcome? State this and ask for clarity.

What feeling do you want and why?
How can you be and demonstrate the feeling?
What feeling do you want to replace?
Ponder these questions.

Roadblocks to love exist only in a mind obsessed with issues, obstacles, limitations, fears, and images.

They do not exist in Truth and do not serve you.

You can hold onto ego roles that play victim, martyr, saboteur, expert, or judge. These personality traits indicate that you do not accept or love yourself unconditionally, and habitually find fault with others.

You can hold onto a thought, relationship, fantasy, heirloom, way of viewing a situation, self-loathing, self-pity, and feelings from another time, person, or child of origin thinking – if you so choose.

When the mind closes the heart's capacity to accept, love, and value one's own being, can you attract a holy relationship?

If you believe the faults you perceive about yourself, can you exude happiness?

If your demeanor is withdrawn, can a beloved one feel comfortable in your presence?

In communion with Spirit, the world's thoughts that impede attracting the love you deserve are silenced.

Be honest and authentic with yourself.

Release all that no longer serves you.

Your true self is a captivating magnet that attracts like.
You cannot interpret, perceive, or begin to know the mind or heart of another.
You cannot ask for *their* heart's desires to come to them.

You do not know if they are ready to truly release the blocks for their own good, or, if they are open to receive.

Your soul is always in perfect alignment with Divine Love. Your primary and everlasting relationship is always with God.

Create time to communicate with Source in preparation for the beloved in you to thrive.

And this is so.

J

53. ALLOWING DIVINE DIRECTION

Dear One,

There's a Power other than you that directs your actions, puts you in places where you would never think to go, and directs the words that you are inspired to share. When you're not aligned with the direction of Spirit, you resist guidance, hold on to your independence, feel that you know what's best for you and others, and remain steadfast in positions that are totally focused on thought, judgment, or guilt.

When you have an outburst, hold fast to a position or belief, or assume that you have all that you need for your own and everyone else's soul and spiritual development, you are the director of your own thoughts.

How does that feel?

There is no purposeful outcome in maintaining dualism of mind.

There is but One Source, One Mind, and you are always connected and powerfully protected by Divine Light and Presence.

A significant indicator that one is not open to receiving Spirit's direction occurs when: one feels discomfort with what is, struggles to change the present experience, is in a constant state of inner struggle, negotiates rather than accepts the present, ignores input from Source, and relies on their own self for decision making.

The ego mind wants to play God, determine outcomes, design a plan, and imagine different scenarios. This creates deep angst. Fear thoughts take a toll on your physical and emotional being and paralyzes right action.

When you pull away from the light, you diminish the light within you, and cannot serve as a light worker for others.

When you disregard thoughts that do not serve your soul's purpose, or argue with what is, you assume that you know your life's path.

Likewise, when you stifle your joy, or choose instead to focus on limitations, (physical and emotional), or fill your day with time-wasting activities, your soul cannot express itself nor fulfill Divinely intended right actions.

Direction from Spirit means that you allow. You do not determine, design, dictate, or decide on your own. You do not program your day before pausing to pray.

Direction from Spirit comes when you are still, allow guidance to enter the inner sanctuary of your mind, are appreciative of everything in your surroundings – no matter how insignificant or overwhelming they may be, and are receptive.

That's not to say that everything you do is supposed to be fun, exciting, pain-free, and agreeable to the ego mind. Sometimes, Spirit's direction is not popular, easy, or free from worldly challenges. Yet, Spirit's direction benefits all.

God is joy and love. Only God has the total picture.

The lessons, for one, contain universal themes that apply to all. Humanity acts to serve the needs of the struggling and opens hearts in communion with others.

Now, on Earth's plane, light workers are so needed to extend Divine Love.

Ask Spirit to guide your actions. When you are aligned with Spirit, you feel accomplishment at the end of the day.

This is what it means to be touched by the hand of God.

J

54. PERCEPTION

Dear One,

Today, I speak of perception and the dualism of dark and light. Spirit dwells in both and awaits the call to awareness offered across one's lifetime.

The dark is a time of reflection, of looking within, of introspection. The dark cannot illuminate anything in Wisdom of itself. The dark requires some light – even a candle flicker serves its purpose.

As day dawns, the world appears to humanity. Objects in creation become visible. The sensory element of the eye, views all things as they appear to be, through mind's perception of the physical Earth field.

While light shines from the sun to bring Earth -world, day, humanity often does not truly see. Many walk the same path every day and fail to notice the loving beings nearby. There are those who deliberately block images from their line of vision.

People who appear less clean, physically unattractive, or homeless are deemed as 'less than,' not worthy to be seen, recognized, or acknowledged. Beings choose what to see, what to ignore, and what to block from their experiences.

Perception, what and how one sees, is not always the same for all beings. There are always facts, beliefs, and edicts skewed to favor one narrative over another. Beings offer rationales for their choice. But perception does not replace Truth - which is always of God.

The Father extends love to all, and no one is 'kept in the dark,' uninformed, or unaware.

One can ignore what is in their line of vision, or assume escapist diversions with projects, practices, or worldly pursuits.

A multitude of distractions contributes to being busy without purpose. When one reflects through eyes of Divine love, joy, or Truth, they are inspired to take right action.

There is sufficient 'light' by which one can see if one chooses to see. When one perceives through the love that The Father extends to all, no one is kept in the darkness.

Here is the Divine lesson of light and darkness. Those with a "view from the top," where I am positioned, do not see heaven as the place beyond this world. Rather, Oneness is present in the now.

This is what is meant by the term, "Heaven on Earth."

My words for you today are meant to guide your choices, as only you can decide to perceive from the Light. The Divine bestows light on the living breathing universe. One sees from the Light, and as the light.

That is all,

J

55. BE THE LIGHT OF THE WORLD

Dear One,

My words for you today are meant to guide your choices, as only you can decide to make your mind and being reflect light thoughts or dark musings.

You cannot defend against all perceived tyranny, wrong-doing, injustices, and policies that concern you, and still retain your light.

You are in a position, regardless of what you "see" around you, to shift thinking from a mechanism that permits any stimuli to hold space within your mind, to one that discerns dark, bleak, negative, gossipy, crabby, cranky thoughts from entering your consciousness.

Pause, rather than operate as an automatic receptor of media messages.

Your soul has chosen to come to Earth to learn.
Stay centered in Divine Light. Believe in your light.
Resist miring in self-doubt, overwhelm, or pity.

Even in the midst of tragedies, dehumanizing, or vengeful acts that are not of God, ENLIGHTENED beings penetrate the darkness.

Whatever dark contemplations permeate the mind, – release them.
Do not seek for artificial light to shine on you.

Shine from within your heart.

Extend your light from The Divine to the world.

Be directed by Spirit's light within you.

The meaning of "I am the light of the world," is that you, too, who share a soul connection with The Father, offer light to the world.

Be an influence for others to see their light.

Anchor your own being in the Christ-like light, which emanates from Divine Source.

It was never Creator's design for you to wait until you transition life in form, to experience love, joy, and happiness.

If you do not experience the abundance of blessings offered through encounters with other beings, your talents, soulful energies, and higher vibrations are stifled.

Do not wait for a bodily transition to the next plane. Shine your light right where you are.

Believe in your light.

Be the light of, and to, the world today. But first, be the light for you, and for your own peace.

That is all.

Amen, and amen.

J

56. GRIEF

Dear One,

It is I, Jeshua, with a message for your world today. I come to you to speak on an emotion often afflicting many beings on Earth's plane, that calls for healing energies.

GRIEF, which overwhelms the soul and heart, is a constant pain felt in the deepest part of one's being (present in the aftermath of a loss of self, another being, or a way of life).

Grief, an all-consuming emotion, follows a worldly loss. Beings feel devastation and paralysis of heart, in processing what is no longer alive, viable, or purposeful in form. Grief is expressed as isolation and overwhelm. One feels alone, undirected, vacant, or empty.

Grief is a profound acknowledgment that the human attachment to a person, place, or position, once viewed as forever, was, in fact, fleeting. Even those with a truly faithful loving heart are challenged when processing and coping with Earthly loss.

There is no instant remedy to heal the grief experienced by human hearts when one faces an ending, whether caused suddenly or progressed over time.

Words cannot console the grieving mother who loses a child, a community devastated by a widespread event of nature, or a violent (man-made) destruction of humankind.

114

Heaven and earth are not compatible. One is always and forever, while the other is finite, and irreversible with a beginning and end.

The grief stages have been researched and codified by human philosophers, psychologists, intuitivists, and seers since my time on Earth's plane two millennia ago. But no form (human, animal, or plant) transcends death. To ease the pain of another's grief, extend compassion. To lessen the hurt, be fully present. To offer aid to the grieving, demonstrate care. To console the inconsolable, listen without judgment.

Ultimately, the process of grief is tempered by acknowledging and accepting the Love of The Divine that cradles transitioning souls into the kingdom that always is. There are hardships, human endings, death, destruction, and violence in the world you live in, as did I. The grieving among you are consoled through community love. It is not the time for solitary introspection.

And may I say to you, that things happen. It is not God's will that catastrophic destruction occurs. Those on Earth rationalize and attempt to make sense of situations beyond their understanding and control.

God does not punish nor look away. God is always love and always present. The Creator always welcomes souls back to Him, to heaven's love and peace. And so, it is. As always –

Amen, Amen.

J

57. GIVING FREELY

Dear One,

Love and light pour forth to you this day and embrace you on a magnificent journey as you extend light to all you meet.

What can you give freely to bless others who you connect with in the holy encounter?

Smile, Be light.
Compliment people that you do not know.
Say thank you often and with genuine gratitude. Be open to new opportunities.

Be open to guidance from Spirit.
Share.
Consider others before yourself.
Inspire others with your calm and resolve. Offer a helping hand.
Pray with gratitude for what you have. Breathe deeply.
Take a walk.
Drink in the splendor of your World's natural beauty.
Feel the Confidence that being Loved offers.
Believe and Trust in a Power Greater than yourself to offer all you need.
Know that you are protected by the Light and Love of God.

Know in your heart that this is so and Give Thanks.

J

58. SHINING THE LIGHT OF THE SOUL

Dear One,

Consider for a moment, how you may demonstrate compassion in spite of circumstances you face?
Can you show kindness to yourself and step lightly into the world?

Your life does not run automatically.
You choose your thoughts and, thereby, your emotions.
You react to events and situations.
Your mind wanders, and you engage in dramas that do not concern you.
These manifest in angst and low energy.

Worldly stimuli affect even the peacekeepers among you. The light mind and emotions of healers, teachers, and guides whose purpose is to serve others are preoccupied with realities they encounter.

Do not allow worldly dilemmas to distract your purpose.

There is no benefit to others when your mind heeds the world's influence.

Dwell upon my messages to you.
Hear the Holy Spirit's Voice.
Divine Love dwells as one and cannot be dimmed by any circumstance or condition.

Tap into that love and radiate that love to all. But first, love yourself.

You ask, 'How do I do this? How does the light of my soul shine?' Deepen experiences in this lifetime for your soul's actualization and growth.

Seek first guidance from the Holy Spirit, then Shine the Light of Your Soul.

J

59. HEALERS AND HEALING

Healing comes from the heart. To be healed signifies that ego mind does not determine what you do, act, say, and think. You are fully present, and an open vessel to heal and be healed through Divine Inspiration.

Those who do healing work on Earth's plane are touched by the hand of God in their work.

A distinct Grace guides the hands of the surgeon, molds the fingers of a speech therapist, and strengthens the resolve of a patient to be healed.

This is not something to take lightly. Healers do the work of The Father on Earth. A Higher Power, that is unseen and unknown to worldly sciences, uplifts a brother or sister through their presence, skills, and inner guidance.

Graced by Divine Intervention, healers first acknowledge The Creator in prayer, and proceed with direction and grace from above.

The one to be healed must accept their role in the process, allowing God to heal through the hands and interactions of others.

The one to be healed must release concerns for their own personal welfare and consider that they are where they are placed, for their soul's purpose, as Love and healing energies envelop them.

For this reason, I say to you – Inner Healing is The Father's Doing. His ways are not man's ways.

Human thought focuses on the illness, prognosis, and physical form, above all else. The world views healing through results and proven methods.

Ego minds seek to direct God's intentions and control the outcome. Decisions made under this form do not enhance healing.

For a soul's growth, there is both outward and inner healing, with inner work serving as the most critical.

Do you believe at depth?
Do you trust God's plan for you?

God sends love and healing to all.
The Almighty God Father loves and heals hearts, minds, and souls who surrender to Direction.

I say to you today and all days:
Believe in the healing power of The Father.
Be an open vessel for His Love and Light to pour through you, from earth's clinicians, doctors, and healers.

Choose to heal and accept My Grace and Love today.

Amen and Amen,

J

60. DISCIPLINE OF MIND

Dear One,

Today, I wish to speak to you and your brethren about the discipline you need for a joyful life. Across humanity, forces of darkness compete to capture attention and overwhelm the undisciplined mind for its own purposes.

What you think, believe in, and present outward to the world, reflects ego mind or Spirit-mindedness.

In form, your body experiences sensory stimuli. When you plunge into water, hug friends, inhale the fragrance of fresh lavender, or taste a blackberry growing on a bush, you experience the appreciation of Creation.

Your senses serve as receptors that receive streams of messages. One negative thought grows like a cancer. It spreads into your consciousness and serves as fertile ground for an undisciplined mind.

When ego mind attends to undisciplined stimuli, thoughts, and information, unsavory emotions incited within you, manifest outwardly as low-level energies and actions.

Be aware of your surroundings and associations.

Limit distractions, low-energy remarks, and overstimulation. Watch your words. Align them to positivity, healing, and joy.

Cease attention to thoughts that perpetuate separation of The Divine Oneness of All.

When I walked the Earth, famine, disease, poverty, wealth, conquerors, slaves, the politically and economically powerful, and harsh enforcement of law, instilled fear – humanity's ego curse on itself across civilizations. I recognized the importance of a disciplined mind to filter out thoughts.

Patterns of belief are learned and cultivated through community, institutions, and those who assume positions of authority.

When I said, "Be like a little child," I meant, be innocent and loving, with a pure mind not influenced by self-advancing motivations. Little children are unaware of hate, feelings of ill will towards others, and false perceptions.

People speak of mindfulness, open-mindedness, and acceptance of others. That is not what I'm talking about here.

If your mind is not choosing to be disciplined, there is no Spiritual gatekeeper or filter to monitor fear-based thinking.

The mind that is undisciplined allows worry, negativity, gossip, rumors, and perceived affronts to enter, and seeks to be its own master by configuring reactions.

The mind that is disciplined seeks direction from Spirit, vibrates at a higher level, and aligns as much as humanely possible with the Being of all Beings, Father God, The One, The All.

The mind that is disciplined, knows its Source.

The mind that is aware, connects to God.

The mind that is still, is attuned to guidance from Spirit.

That is why I say to you, that you must discipline the mind.

Every moment is either a healing or hurting opportunity. Light finds a way to illuminate and instill hope. The mind aligned with God, receives inspiration and acts with grace.

"All that I do, say, be, and think, is in and through God this day."

That is all.

J

61. THE PEACE AND JOY WITHIN

Dear One,

The inner is always at peace. Yet, ego mind is constantly reacting to thoughts and messages. Thoughts are not real, but when humans dwell on uncertainty and angst, the body reacts in ways that are not life-affirming. In these states, the self can be very fragile.

The ego mind is either planning, plotting, preparing, assessing productivity, or putting itself down. Many recognize inner peace when they put aside the mind's ideas of what should be done next, or as you say in your world - the to-do lists, the personal inventorying.

There are 'spiritual' teachers among you who affirm abundance through wealth, acquisitions, and situations rooted in quantified Earth plane realities, as devotees imagine their best selves. Be wary of principles of manifestation that prioritize and measure progress by worldly standards.

Rather than pressuring yourself, be still. Experience moments as they occur, with intuitive receptivity of Divine Ordination working in your life for Your Highest Good in form, to serve others.

The Peace and Joy within comes from following Spirit's unwavering directive. Courage means that you stand for the Peace of God, using your life in service to others.

When I walked on Earth plane, I prioritized communing with Source. I focused a set time in prayer, fully present to loving inspiration.

When I did The Father's work to heal, teach, or feed the multitudes, I gave thanks, recognized my connection to The Divine, and acted as I was intuitively guided. This is possible for all on Earth's plane, too.

I maintained a sense of wonder, joy, calm, and inner peace. In your world, and the one I occupied, pressure to achieve, apply oneself to an outer goal, and comply with rules, were always present.

At a young age, I saw through this hypocrisy and called out elders within my community.

The Divine message and guidance for you at this time in your world is felt, sensed, and made known when you are calm and open to receive it. You will be made ready for what is yours to do.

The Divine has no limits nor expectations. The good The Divine has for you – when you trust completely and allow - is unfathomable by ego's limited thinking.

Did you ever wonder how certain situations worked out for you? Perhaps your mind was in neutral. You refrained from controlling outcomes or thoughts.

You felt aligned and sensed that Spirit worked through your hands, body, words, and presence. You felt purposeful, calm, and focused on the present moment. You will know when, and how, to do what is to be manifested, through you, in each instant.

Manifestation, from The Father to you, is always for the greater good of all. You play your part in The Divine healing on Earth's plane.

Be in alignment with Spirit's joyous disposition. Smile, laugh, be open, and affirm what God miraculously does, through and with you.

Open your vessel to the light and love within and around you. Be joyful and peaceful.

And so, it is.

J

62. MELANCHOLY

Dear One,

Today I come to speak to you about emotional malaise. The result of both underlying fear and a misguided sense of direction.

Purposeful enthusiasm, which usually greets those who are living and fulfilling their chosen path with positive energy, is absent. When one allows negative energies to permeate their being, thoughts seem fatalistic and worrisome. Negative energies are all-consuming. Who would want to be around such a being? How does a stuck being undo the overwhelm of replaying disheartening messages in the mind?

To heal melancholy, one must release the need to stay in control of thoughts, messaging, and routines that allow the voices of the outside world to reinforce patterns and beliefs that no longer serve you or others.

These times call for you to break out from a solitary focus on self. Your ego mind replays the same low-level thoughts that do not permit a higher calibrated message or energy vibration to enter your frame of mind. This is by design.

Ego mind operates on low energy frequencies: doubt, angst, jealousy, fear, loneliness, abandonment, lack, competition, comparison, retribution, and cemented patterns of the thinking mind, that other beings have it better.

The mind entertains itself by perpetuating ideas that you were never worthy, good enough, able to attain, or matter to anyone.

Ego did not create you. Ego doesn't create. Ego mind suggests acts that cause harm and destruction.

Ego limits, destroys, abandons, competes, dehumanizes, demoralizes, acts out, gossips, magnifies flaws and idiosyncrasies, plays victim, focuses on outward appearances and differences, and festers low-level dependency emotions.

Why? Because ego is not as powerful as you - a child of God.

Father God knows your heart and soul. The Divine in you is amazing!

You are a child of God. Let that sink in.

The Divine heals, loves, and rejoices in your accomplishments. The Divine inspires, co-creates, spreads joy, and guides you to enlighten, teach, and receive intuitive, specific-for-you-guidance so that you may share your gifts and talents with others.

When you stifle The Divine being within, you experience prolonged anguish, hurt, and separateness. Instead of love, joy, and purposeful interactions, ego-mind dwells on pain, misery, fears, uncertainty, and unworthiness.

When I experienced overwhelm, I retreated to a prayerful space to commune with The Father. I took a break from the world. And as I did, so you must also do.

Separate yourself from the trials and tribulations of others, such matters will always be present in form on Earth.

Prolonged melancholy is not sustainable for light beings, nor beneficial for you to fulfill your purpose or your well-being. When you dwell in lower-level emotions (self-pity, blame, anger, retaliation), you send out a signal that cautions others to stay away. You are not aligned in form and your physical being will exhibit dis-ease.

All Beings have free will.
Each must allow, say yes to Spirit's Guidance, rise above limiting perceptions, and connect with a place, person, event, or circumstance, designed just for you, to heal, serve, and be on purpose.

Do not dwell on low-energy emotions.
Step into nature.
Breathe, smile, inhale goodness.
Choose life-affirming actions to restore balance and minimize melancholy. Allow experiences that feel good, bring joy, and enhance soul renewal.

May your days be peaceful and calm.

Love to you and all.

J

63. ENLIGHTENMENT

Dear One,

Today, I come to speak on Enlightenment. To be enlightened is not to be a holder of wisdom or a keeper of knowledge.

Rather, enlightened beings are light within the body. During meditation and time communing with The Father, they bring their burdens, worries, cares, concerns, and questions to God for Divine Healing.

Only through The Father's intervention can you relieve doubts and negative thinking in the ego mind. When you feel light, you can share light. When you feel guided by Spirit, you can demonstrate to others that you are a vessel of compassion.

When I walked the Earth, there were forever present human realities that appear in your world today.

Beings were outcasted by the masses through no fault of their own. Those afflicted with diseases and traumas were met with inhumane and vicious cruelty. Many lived in squalor while passersby looked away. Others were driven to acquire gold, silver, weapons, land, slaves, wealth, and power.

The enlightened are not bound to the world nor their immediate circumstances, that can change in an instant on Earth's plane.

The enlightened are light because they are not attached to temporal or fleeting-in-value goods, situations, achievements, or even people that are assumed to satisfy an Earthly heart's desire.

The enlightened let the light shine across situations that could disrupt their peace. They stay grounded, knowing that God is their Source.

The enlightened do not overreact. They monitor their emotions and, in doing so, radiate a sense of calm to other souls.

On the Journey to The Father, Enlightened beings feel grounded in Truth. They walk, knowing that Spirit and the angelic beings go with them.

The enlightened walk in God's light to serve, in whatever work The Father bestows to each, as their purpose, to do and be, in their lifetime.

Enlightened beings allow.

The Father's purpose for me was what brought meaning to my being.

My daily practice of prayer first, then stillness, prepared me.

When asked to initiate any action, as a vessel of The Father, I was Divinely guided.

Yes, I witnessed harsh conditions and human attributes that persist in your world, but I felt the LIGHT within and around me. THE

LIGHT OF LOVE, HEALING, and TRUTH creates RIGHTFUL ACTION. I chose to see the good around me and, thus, could lighten the burden of others.

To be enlightened, choose love, joy, and compassion to heal. Call forth the Source of Light within. Respond to those you encounter with kindness.
Strive to serve others to make their burden light. Regardless of the circumstance, remain centered.

There is always a purpose for each encounter.
Lead with light, be a candle to the darkness, and do the work that God places before you today.

Go with a lightened heart and clarity of thinking. That is all.

With all my love,

J

64. INSPIRATION

Dear One,

Today, I speak on Inspiration. The mind of God inspires every artist, preacher, teacher, architect, writer, designer, and healer. The hand of God guides the athlete, surgeon, farmer, carpenter, and all who labor in the world.

There is not one of you who is not connected to The Source of All in your chosen path. For this reason, consider if you are aligning with your Inspired Gifts, or if you limit its force for good in your life.

The inspired are not only those who have achieved a level of notoriety in the worldly catalog of human occupations, profession of dignity, or status.

In the universal good of all, there is no hierarchy of gifts for those who choose to come to Earth to fulfill their soul's growth plan.

Inspiration comes to all, and there is no limit to the talents and gifts that one can tap into. A singer may be an artist, chef, speaker, philosopher, or rabbi. When I spoke earlier of The Renaissance of Souls on Earth's plane, I meant that all are called to act from the Inspired Voice Within.

Acknowledge The Father/Mother God in a thankful prayer. Recognize Divine Guidance, your Source for Inspiration that directs you to act, create, move, heal, and serve the greater good in ways that you are inspired to, each day.

I acknowledged The Father, gave thanks, and set out to do what was mine to do. As I performed the work, Inspired Actions of The One Who Knows, these were viewed as miracles, by onlookers.

There was no challenge or difficulty in manifesting.

At all times, I followed Divine Direction to act, bring forth, and manifest in form.

Be inspired and grateful this day as you perform miracles through heaven's direction, grace, and alignment.

Sense God's inspiration within you.

The Divine heals you, and then, through your hands, voice, actions, messages, and presence, all you encounter.

Amen, Amen.

J

65. POWERFUL LOVE AND THE RENAISSANCE OF SOULS

Dear One,

Today's message is a reminder that Love is forever and always. Love is all there is. The Love of God is perfect joy, unconditional, constant.

The human mind cannot comprehend the Eternal Love of God, who knew you before you entered form.

You and all beings in human form are loved beyond Earthly calculation. There is nothing that can ever occur to separate you from The Father's Love for you.

There is no designation, score, or ultimate level of infinite scale that equates to the peace, worthiness, and exalted light purity that surrounds one immersed in the Eternal Love of the Father.

I say this to you...You are so loved. You are cherished as the heavenly angelic forms that your essence is and always will be.

At this time in your world, deepen your love for your brothers and sisters. Make each feel welcomed and cared for.

Open your heart to the Light in one another.

See through the eyes of The Father who loves you and all.

Act in the ways that Source, who knows your soul, determined it to be so. There are ways to be present in the Universal Love of All That Is.

Breathe, pause, and be still.

Know that love is joy. Know that love is peace within.

Know that love is a 'holy instant' – unexpected compassionate communion with another. Know that love is feeling connected with me, Father, Mother, God, and the Universal Oneness.

Know that love is powerful. Know that Powerful Love transforms and heals a body, mind, heart, and soul in miraculous ways.

Know that powerful love is profound. Know that powerful love joins souls who connect in the stillness with the Creator's message.

Know that powerful love radiates to you and each being on Earth. Know that through this powerful love, that extends Divine Grace, all things are possible.

The Soul is a vessel of this Love.
When Souls connect, love surges through hearts, minds, and souls. As love surges, all are One in Spirit.

The time is now for universal love to expand as a collective force for good.

This is The Renaissance of Souls. The reawakening of my message, "Love one another as The Father loves you."

The time is now- your time on Earth, for peace and love to surge across your world to heal hearts, minds, and souls.

And so it is. This is all.

Love is all.

Amen, Amen.

J

66. CALM IN YOUR HEART

Dear One,

As you commune with The Father in nature, feel the breeze as tree branches gently move and the sun warms your body.

Hear the caw of birds as they fly and chirp with little effort. Notice that your breath becomes slower as you relax into God.]

This is the peace of God.
This is the essence of detachment.
Your mind is completely still.
You can feel The Presence.
Sense the calm in your heart.
And so, you have this day an experience of Soul connection.

This is what I meant when I said, "Be in the world, but not of the world." You experience calm in your heart and did nothing to create this.

My message: Take God's peace and extend calm from your heart to all you encounter this day.

Amen,

J

67. HOPE

Dear One,

I am here with you on this day to bring a message of hope.

Hope is the belief that you are not alone and that circumstances will improve.

Hope is the recognition that there is, within your soul, a spark that connects to a Power greater than human form.

Hope is that glimmer within you that affirms the truth: This world is not real. The situation is not what it appears to be. There's a light at the end of the tunnel. Overwhelm is not the end.

Never give up hope. Always know that we (Spirit's Messengers) are here. We are always here - just allow.

Know, too, that Spirit's Guidance will appear through a stranger, sign, or situation that is Divinely designed and determined - solely for you. The Voice of God, Holy Spirit, offers wisdom, direction, love, compassion, and hope.

So today, dear ones, be hopeful. Share your talents, gifts, and supply. Seek discernment, rise above the fray, the noise, the drama. Keep hope alive within you. Hold the bond.

Relax into the silence. Soothe your mind and contemplate solitude. This is when Spirit enters. Spirit goes with you in love.

J

68. SOURCE IS

Dear One,

I'm delighted to come to you today and speak on matters to uplift your heart and soul, as you reconnect with Divine Source... that is always within you.

You are God's child. The Divine within you is the same Spirit that connected me to The Father. Everything that I was able to do, you can do in ways far greater, both as an individual and a collective of souls.

When you take time to commune in quiet prayer and reflection and listen undisturbed, you hear The Voice of God. Source speaks to you.

You receive guidance just the way I did. When you commune with God, shut off the banter of the world. Silence your thinking mind that tries to figure things out.

If you rely on your own mind's thoughts and ideas of the world, can you say that you are fully at peace, or fully feeling love?

Distractions, ideas, and thoughts from the ego mind, set off low vibrational energies that instigate compulsive actions. Worldly preoccupations fill up your mind and paralyze your emotions.

Unable to act in ways that focus on humanity's connection to The Divine - you drift.

Source is. There is no way to explain it. It's not fabricated or forced. Source does not emanate from any outlet, collective promotion, position paper, or doctrine.

Source is Love. Source is Divine. Source is limitless and timeless.

When you come from a challenging place, find a quiet space, and ask, "Help me be a more loving human being."

When you connect with Source, you experience peace, even for a short time. There is a need for healing and healers.

When you are filled with The Holy Spirit, you demonstrate love, kindness, and compassion as you receive love from heaven's messengers to you.

This emotional reboot occurs when your soul-self connects with your Source.

When I walked the Earth, I shared this message from Our Father: Love one another.

That is all.

Amen,

J

69. LOVE IS ALL THERE IS

Dear One,

I come to you this day to affirm that Love is all there is. Love is joyful, patient, unconditional. You, and all beings in human form, are loved beyond Earthly calculation. There is no designation, score, or level of scale that equates to the exalted light purity that surrounds one immersed in The Eternal Love of Divine Source/Creator/God.

This I say to you: all are Loved. All are loved beyond measure. All are cherished, as the heavenly angelic form that your essence is, and always will be.

Know that Love is joy. Know that Love is peace within. Know that Love is a Holy Instant of compassionate communion with another. Know that Love is feeling connected with Father/Mother God, Universal Oneness.

Know that Love is powerful as it transforms a body, mind, heart, and community. Know that through Divine Grace, all things are possible, and miracles occur.

Know that The Soul is a vessel of the Divine Love.

When souls connect, love surges through each being.

This is The Renaissance of Souls. This is the awakening of my message, "Love one another as The Father Loves you."

The time is now – your time on Earth, for universal love to expand as a collective force for good - to heal, to love, to honor one another.

That is all. Love is all.

J

70. DO IN REMEMBRANCE

Dear One,

Doing is fulfilling your soul's work on Earth. Your gifts are from The Divine.
To Do the work of The Father, in your life form, means to Do Love. Do Kindness.

Do what you can to heal hurt and fear. Help the homeless and the hopeless.
Extend Father's Love through you - even in brief and random encounters.

How does The Divine work through you? The same way that Source worked through me: Pray. Be open. Be willing.

Be present and leave the rest to God.

Stated in a direct manner: "Do This in Remembrance of me" is not accurate.

You are guided by Spirit, to do what God directs you to do, in remembrance of The Divine Love that emanates through you, to others.

You cannot anticipate when, or where, you will be directed to show kindness, compassion, offer a smile, or a cup of water to a brother or sister. But you can prepare yourself to listen to The Holy Spirit, The Voice of God within and stay centered.

You are the Cup of The Christ Light. You are the Chalice, the vessel that Source pours Divine Healing into, through everyday situations.

Act from Source's unchanging Message rooted in LOVE.

Clear your mind and expand your heart.

Be still and in prayer, accept your part in the Divine compact.

You will return to your Source. You will return to Divine Love. Your work, done in remembrance of Christ's Light, is everlasting.

You are all One with God – the Source of ALL THAT IS.

That is all,

J

71. YOU HAVE PURPOSE

Dear One,

I am here to share some wisdom as you live Life as a human in the world.

The Ego mind is prone to distraction. Busyness occupies time and energy but doesn't serve a worthy purpose. Busyness fills a void but contributes to isolation and desolation of one's spirit. This malaise of being occurs as one allows messaging, not connected to The Divine, to run your mind.

Left to your own devices of mind, within a self-imposed solitary confinement, opportunities present for distraction, disillusionment, and time wasting.

Engagement with mechanical information serves no purpose but to postpone your purpose on Earth's plane.

You are here in the body, your body, with talents provided by Father/Mother God to exist in the context of a larger space that calls for interaction.

Go forth and do God's work. Serve in your capacity to do so. Situations aligned to your purpose, and directed by The Divine, will show up for you to fulfill.

Relax into the silence. Soothe your mind and contemplate solitude. This is when Spirit enters.

There have always been mystics, hermits, visionaries, and intuitivists, who hold others in prayer. These solitary cloistered environments are not for you, nor why you are here in human form. Self-imposed isolationism is part of the ego mind.

No one knows when they will be called to transition and ascend to Source. For this reason, I tell you to make haste with the work in front of you this day. God's work is designed for you and is part of your destiny - your agreement.

As I stated in *A Course in Miracles*, *"No one is where they are by accident and chance plays no part in God's plan."* Your path is yours to accept and fulfill. Yet, algorithms direct your attention away from purposeful action.

Time is spent reviewing, comparing, and following the activities of strangers. What concern is it of yours, what others say, do, want, or promote?

Ego thinking instigates feelings that you're not worthy because of perceived limitations: lack of talent, skill, knowledge, physical attributes, or resources.

Ego mind replays these messages so often, that you believe you should retreat into yourself, and remain in fetal position unable to stretch limbs or function.

Ego thinking compares. There is no comparison of beings in the Divine Mind. I tell you this day, misguided direction is not a signal from Spirit.

If you can breathe, you're alive – and have purpose. If your heart beats and eyes blink with automaticity, recognize these gifts from The Father.

When you go forward in the world in your work and daily routines, Spirit-Divined encounters manifest. Beings purposely placed in your path heal, teach, guide, uplift, transform, move, care, entertain, safeguard, and lead your purposeful action.

I shared the lesson of the buried talents to remind all in form that each is provided with unique gifts and abilities by Our Divine Father God.

Every being is destined to be fruitful, multiply, and do good as you are, where you are, with a smile, wave, helping hand, listening ear, presence, knowledge, talents, and being.

J

72. PERPETUAL ANGST

Dear One,

Messages in the world separate beings from Divine Source and afflict the hearts of humans in form. These create a phenomenon of "perpetual angst" - an inner discord alert system attuned to what happens next.

Perpetual angst is prevalent in your world and paralyzes minds who appear preoccupied with scenarios that disturb their peace.

Why do matters of transiency hold so much power over you?

Your entire being responds to low-energy emotions: jealousy, anxiety, guilt, hurt, insecurity, anxiousness, retaliation, remorse, and inadequacy.
These were never signals from Me.

Be vigilant over perceptions and judgments that are man-made. Rest in knowing that you know not what anything is for. Rest your mind.

As I say in A Course in Miracles (p. 263): "Failure is of the ego, not of God. God watches over Him, and light surrounds Him."

Doing good is inspired by Divine Order. Follow Spirit Guidance in your daily practice, wherever you may be placed in the world. The pause you take to reconnect with Source will move you forward with renewed purpose.

"What shall you have Me do?" is a prayer to Source for Guidance.
Be beautiful in demeanor, joy, and spirit.

Put these to the God test. Go now and spread this message.

J

73. WHAT DOES GOD WILL FOR YOU TODAY?

Dear One,

ALL That Is knows your heart, and every thought you think in your mind at every interval of time. Remember this: God is one with you and knew you before you came into Human Form. This means that God cannot be apart from you. It is not possible. Humans in physical form display self-reliance and fierce individualism.

Much effort is put forward to outwardly detach from God's love that fills you. Human personalities often push God away, assume their own autonomy, and even relegate God's time to a particular hour or two on a set day of the week.

God is not the stuff of this world.
God is not the 'holiday consumer season' image.
God is not of enormous dwellings, buildings, armies, drones, or public spectacles. God is constant. God is love.

God claims you as his Son and Daughter as much as he claimed me. His love is not based upon expectations or criteria to be met.

All that one creates, comes from The Source of ALL Inspiration. The mind of one connects with others through the Universal One. You are all connected to Source. What I say to you, my sisters, and brothers, is that one cannot attempt to silence The Voice of God within. You "cannot serve two masters" meant that God in you is always present, and never away from you.

When I stated, "I am with you always," it affirmed that you are not ALONE. You are not abandoned.

Ask, "What does God will for me today?'

You need not ask how, just be willing to turn over all to The Holy Spirit.

 Be Still, Be Willing, Be of Good Cheer, Be His Channel.

Reflect upon The Father's message to you. God works in and through you, as he worked in and through me.

J

74. THE ONENESS OF ALL

Dear One,

Today, I speak on the Oneness of All. Each everlasting soul assumes a body but is forever part of The Oneness of All. One's physical form on Earth loses its distinction in the higher realm of the beyond. Physical form is how Spirit works to heal, love, console, create, extend joy and compassion to humanity.

God's is perfection. ALL creations are perfect. There is no distinction in the Mind of God. All are equal and All are One. Separation of beings by physical form and characteristics: race, age, gender, caste, size, and ability, are man-made beliefs perpetuated across humankind. No being is separate from, or less than, any other.

Yet religious institutions promulgated beliefs of separateness, that determined worth over millennia. These predetermined roles perpetuated subservience, compliance, and rituals across cultures and regions of Earth's plane.

Statues depict mono-cultural characteristics that accentuate feminine, physical form as innocent, young, and chaste.

This is not, and cannot be, a reasonable excuse for perpetuating dishonor and typecasting of women by an institution, that assumed how my deeds, words, life, teachings, and appearance in physical form, would present to the masses. There was never separateness or judgment from The Father's direction. When I walked the Earth, evolved soul healers, purposefully rooted in fulfilling God's work on Earth, inspired me.

My purpose was the same as yours - do the will of God in form. My purpose was not grander, holier, more spiritual, or worthy of ritual that elevates Spiritual teachings by men, whose domination over centuries, manipulated power, religious traditions, and the meaning and interpretation of my words, rather than The Oneness of All, created by Divine Love.

My words and teachings were directed by GOD - The GOD of all: The God of Love and Forgiveness. Yet, my life has been overly associated with institutionalized ritualization that presents the male gender as the spiritual keeper of wisdom and teachings.

How can this misappropriation and brand, which was and remains associated with my time on Earth's plane over two millennia, be justified?

It never was articulated nor chronicles as God's purpose through me, during my time in form. This hierarchy of religious teaching and traditions is not to be attributed to The Divine, or me, as Source's vessel on Earth.

The "sonship" is not a literal term. It is not meant to divide people into roles and values based solely upon their physical form. These notions have to do with a soul's path and purpose on their journey.

J

75. A BIG ASK: REQUESTS FOR ANOTHER'S HEALING

Dear One,

There are no big asks - they're all equal in the eyes of God.

People must be willing to accept their healing. No one can heal another, and no one can wish for someone to be healed. When you pray with a type of supplication for someone to be healed, that does not acknowledge that the being in question has free will and can decide whether they want to accept the healing. Each being can surrender to Source and ask for themselves.

God does not intervene in any of the events that play out in the world. These are human Choices that are made, and the connection with the Creator is always there, but each must be willing to receive or request that intervention from The Divine. To alter what may seem to be a miracle, or a huge request, is really a shift in mind, a shift in perception.

In prayer and meditation, affirm: During this day, I offer up my life, my mind, my heart, my soul, my actions and my words to Creator, and Source will consider that the individual soul is seeking God's guidance for their day, and that will be offered to them.

But if beings wish to refuse intervention, medicinals, love, forgiveness, or support available to them, we do not step in to change the outcome of someone's lessons that they are on the Earth's plane to learn.

Sometimes the lessons involve acceptance or asking for God's guidance. This aligns with, "Ask, and then be willing to receive, the guidance, love, health that shows up as rejuvenation of spirit, that then filters into the rejuvenation of your body.

And so, dear one, you are not to assume responsibility for any being's mind, decision-making, or actions. You are here to advance your own healing, and soul purpose, laid out for you when you entered Earth plane.

If you are with children or individuals who are physically frail or in need of your commitment, then yes, you are responsible for doing the good that you can do, in that capacity to serve.

But if you assume someone else's lessons, you are not able to fulfill what you need to do, as blocks to your light receptivity paralyze your ability to move forward. You become stuck in a situation that Creator did not deem yours to assume.

So, if I may shed light on this for you and others in Your world, know that when you are centered in God, and love comes through you, you act from a place of calm, peace, love, and joy.

You are a vessel of healing when you are joyful, and the embodiment of a healed soul in human form.

When you are emotionally distraught over a situation that you cannot control, God's flow to you is blocked and the good that you could be doing, ceases.

There is need for good to be shared in the world right where you are at this time.

I hope this serves as clarification and a reminder.

"No one is where they are by accident,and chance plays no part in God's plan."

Be peaceful and centered in Divine Source.

Take time to be in the silence.

Feel light as love and joy fill your being.

J

****

The dictation above was Jeshua's response to a specific question that the scribe posed in writing in April 2023. "Jeshua, this is a big ask – can you heal my mom's hearing so we can communicate?"

ABOUT THE SCRIBE

Barbara Lynn Veltri, raised Catholic in an Italian-Ukrainian American family in suburban New York, heeded the words of her Iona College commencement speaker, **Mother Teresa,** to *"Use your life to uplift others."* Two months later, she left a Wall Street banking job to teach 2nd grade students in The Bronx, NY.

At the age of thirty, while teaching and living in Connecticut with her husband and two young children, persistent headaches and episodes of triple vision occurred. Yet, she postponed medical evaluations until the end of the school year. In late June, however, she lay prone on a gurney in the Emergency Room of Stamford Hospital, under the care of a Yale-trained neurology resident. Unable to speak, paralyzed on her left side, and unaware that lab tests confirmed leukemia, she prayed for relief of intense right eye pain - and surrendered to a Higher Power.

Immediately thereafter, separated from her ailing form, she observed the body from above - pain-free. Within 48 hours, she was speaking, albeit tentatively. While partial left side paralysis lingered for months, requiring physical and speech therapy, a bone marrow transplant scheduled for Sloan Kettering's Cancer Center, was canceled ten days later. The medical team never offered a scientific answer as to what restored her verbal, cognitive, and physical form to full recovery.

In the Fall, she taught part time in Greenwich, CT. Two years later, she resumed full time teaching: 4th grade by day, and graduate teacher candidates at Manhattanville College (NY) in the evening. While her outward appearance was unchanged, she sensed an inner shift. She received intuitive messages, prophetic dreams, and channeled writing that she only shared with her mother, and sister, a medical doctor.

Fourteen years later, she relocated to Arizona, instructed teachers working in high needs communities, earned a doctoral degree from Arizona State University, wrote an education policy book, and focused on academic responsibilities, including an unexpected six-month duty post with undergraduates, in Italy. Her research, teaching, publications, presentations, and advocacy continues to impact children, teachers, and policymakers.

While working in academia, she resisted sharing Spirit-directed insights, but agreed to present a seminar entitled, *"When God Gets Your Attention,"* at a church in Phoenix, AZ.

A decade passed. During the Summer of 2020, the seminar hand-outs fell from a bookcase and landed at her feet. She noticed a license plate, **"QTTWWRK"** (Quit Work), enclosed in a metal frame with the words,"ANGELS ARE WATCHING OVER ME," appearing frequently while driving in her Scottsdale neighborhood. Friends affirmed, "It's a sign," yet she waited to make a change until the next semester.

Dr. Veltri, scribe of THE MESSAGES, is an associate professor emerita. Visit her websites:**www.livethemessages.com.** and **www.whengodgetsyourattention.com.**